REAL SELF:

THE INNER JOURNEY OF COURAGE

REAL SELF:

THE INNER JOURNEY OF COURAGE

SANDRA J. MERWIN

TigerLily Press
Minnetonka, Minnesota

ISBN: 0-9628522-0-1

10 9 8 7 6 5 4 3 2 1

Printed in the United States of America

In this book female and male pronouns are used alternately chapter by chapter. My examples are from my life experiences. The details of examples have been changed in order to honor other's boundaries and prevent identification.

*To Ralph Cook, who completed his life journey
November 12, 1989.*

Contents

Acknowledgements

I am deeply appreciative to my clients and colleagues who shared their stories with me.

I want to acknowledge the important support and encouragement I received from those people who listened: Jason Cook, Roberta Morrison, Anne Graves, Karalyn Harrington, Rich Meiss, Mary Stultz and Anne Sturdivant.

I also want to thank Andrew, who helped me test-pilot the map.

Introduction

I started this book at least a hundred times. I've written it and rewritten it in my head at least twenty times in the last year. I capture the essence of what I want to say, then as soon as I write the phrase, the true essence of what I want to say begins to fade. So, please read between the words and listen with your heart to hear the song behind the words. All the words do is point the way. You must look beyond the words to see the truth.

1

The Journey

As the body died, the spirit rose above the dying form. And as the spirit continued to rise, it encountered the Great Spirit, who gently asked, "While you journeyed on earth, did you sing your own song?"

In the journey on earth, have you chosen to sing your own song? A song is the melody for expressing the intense personal experience of who you are. The journey on earth is an old metaphor that describes human life as a personal history with a beginning, a middle and an end. It is true that all human beings share three experiences: they are born, they die and they have a limited time on earth. This limited time on earth is referred to as the "life journey."

These life journeys vary greatly and no one can know what your life journey will include or require. Yet, the life journey metaphor can be very useful for gaining an understanding of practical ways of approaching living.

If you were going on a vacation, you'd have an idea of where you wanted to go, who you'd want to take with you and how you were going to get there. Even if you just chose to get in the car and drive, you'd still have to make a choice about which direction to head. Regardless of whether you are a planner, who wants your whole vacation mapped out or you are a free spirit who wants to just get in the car and drive, you still have to make choices. The planner will make the choices sooner. The free spirit will wait to see what is happening and then make the choice at the moment, but sooner or later both will have to make choices about what direction to head and how to get there.

Viewing the life journey as having the common elements of any journey offers us the opportunity to reach a viewing point. This viewing point is like looking out the window of an airplane as it flies over a large city. You can see the patterns of streets and highways and houses. Even though you may have driven those streets and highways a hundred times, you still will experience a new, larger aerial view of the city.

For any journey, a map is helpful and of course it's easier if you can speak the language. This book is designed so that you have the opportunity to see the most recent map of the life journey that I can create. I have found this map to be dynamic; as I grew and developed, I noticed that the map subtly changed. You will want to make the map fit your life. So, feel free to add to the map until it fits you. The language I offer you in the following chapters is a language that will give you words to talk about what you need, what you believe and who you are. I've had to make up a few words. The English language I speak left me with concepts that I couldn't describe with the words I had at hand.

So, lets take an aerial view of the life journey. Remember no one can know exactly what your life will entail, but there is a good chance that you will be able to use the following elements to develop an awareness of why you make the choices you do and who you are.

Figure 1 represents the aerial view of a life journey map. It shows the inner journey of growth and development which each human has the opportunity to travel. The journey begins at the circle labeled Original Self. Original Self is who we were at birth when we arrived, predisposed with genetic material already forming the pattern for what we could be in the future.

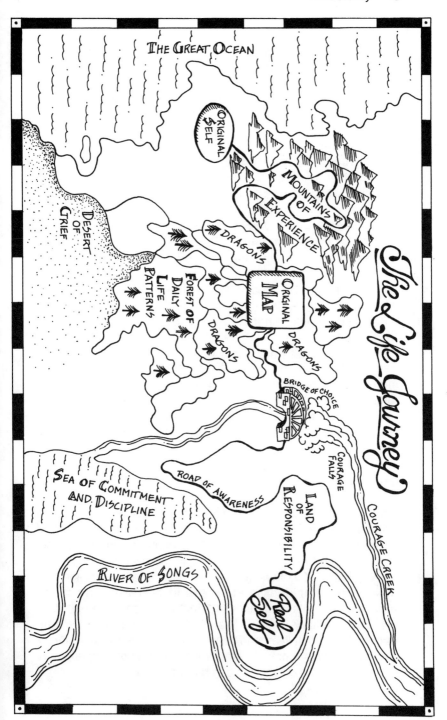

Figure 1

Starting at Original Self and moving from left to right you will notice the word "experiences." These are the first experiences we have as children. These experiences form the basis for our first understanding of the world. People who have carefully looked at their Original Maps report that their first beliefs about the world could be stated:

"The world isn't safe."

"I always have to hurry."

"I am always hungry."

"When I'm hungry, there is food for me."

"The world is a warm, loving place."

"I don't belong here."

"The people here love me."

From these first experiences, each of us tries to make sense of the world. Each child experiences what happens when he cries or gets angry. Over time, the child determines the behaviors he must use to survive and get his needs met. Out of these first experiences, the child creates his first map of the world. The first map becomes the foundation for all future experiences.

As I've collected information for this book, I have been amazed to find that many of us share common childhood experiences. One person told me that when she cried at school the Nuns stood her in front of the room so everyone could see the "cry baby." Another person told me his teacher made him crawl under her desk and sit at her feet when he made mistakes. These experiences are very common. They are part of each individual's Original Map. These experiences become roadblocks in adult lives and cause voices to falter when they try to sing their own songs. I want to share one of my experiences with you since the only truth I can really tell is my own.

It's been 32 years since it happened. I still remember it and can replay it like my own home video. I think it's a story about Roberta, but I know it's also about me.

Roberta and I were six and a half years old. I remember because both our birthdays fell in the middle of November. We were in first grade. At recess, Roberta was always first because she could run fast. Her long black braids, which normally rested on her chest, would stand out behind her when she ran, as if they were trying to keep up with her.

When I was six and a half I liked animals better than anything else. I begged my father to buy me a horse. I already had a cat and a dog and I had watched all the Disney animal movies at least twice. *National Velvet* and *Bambi* were my favorites. *Old Yeller* was too sad. So it's no surprise to me that I thought of people as animals. I was a cat. Roberta was a doe.

Roberta had large brown eyes which were offset by the high Indian cheekbones of her Blackfoot heritage.   When we were on the playground she could jump and run better than any of the other first graders, but in the classroom she was quiet and shy. She seemed smaller when she was inside the school. She never raised her hand and she spoke so quietly that the teacher had to bend over next to Roberta's desk and strain to hear her answers.

Miss Barker was our teacher. She wore her dark hair in miniature ponytail on the top of her head. Miss Barker was exciting and fun and safe. She was a new college graduate and was making up for her lack of experience with enthusiasm. Everyone in our class loved Miss Barker, not only because she was so energetic and concerned about us, but because we were afraid of the other first grade teacher, Mrs. Horvick, who was old and talked in a demanding high pitched voice. Whenever I heard her voice, even if she wasn't talking to me, my body would become tense and still as I tried to become smaller than I was. She always wore high heeled shoes that thundered down the hall when she walked. Miss Barker reminded me of a rabbit. I never figured out which animal Mrs. Horvick reminded me of. In fact I never thought about Mrs. Horvick at all if I could help it.

After the first parent teachers conference, I heard my mother explain to my father, "since Miss Barker was fresh out of college, Mrs. Horvick was the supervisor of both first grade classes." This made my mother feel more confident about my education. It made my stomach feel fluttery.

I think it was during reading that I first noticed Miss Barker's distress. Roberta would not read out loud. When Miss Barker asked her to read from our *Dick and Jane* book, Roberta only shook her head and looked down at her desk. Then when Roberta thought Miss Barker wasn't looking, she would look out the window at the cottonwood trees. But Miss Barker usually noticed and sighed heavily before she would say, "Roberta, please keep your attention on your work."

Reading was always after noon recess. At recess one afternoon, Roberta told me her father, who was a chief, bought her a pinto pony. I was so envious that I didn't choose her to be on my kickball team which meant that the other team won the game.

When we filed into the classroom I looked for Roberta to tell her I was sorry I hadn't chosen her, but I couldn't find her. The bell rang and her desk stayed empty. I raised my hand and when Miss Barker called my name I said, "Roberta's gone. She didn't come back from recess." Her voice trembled a little when she said, "Yes, I know. Class, please open your reading books."

Reading class continued as it always did except I stumbled over the words more than usual when it was my turn to read. Reading was almost over when Mrs. Horvick marched in holding Roberta by one thin brown arm. Mrs. Horvick towered over Roberta, who appeared even smaller than usual. My body tensed and my stomach began to hurt. No one in the room moved, as Mrs. Horvick said in her shrill voice, "Roberta has agreed to read out loud, isn't that right Roberta." Hair falling from a loose braid covered her face as she stood paralyzed, staring at the floor. "Isn't that right, Roberta!" Mrs. Horvick shrilled as she shook Roberta by her thin brown arm.

Roberta took a shuddering breath broken with deep sobs. Mrs. Horvick shook her once again. "Answer me,

Roberta. Are you going to read out loud for Miss Barker?" The quavering "yes" came between choked breathing and sobbing. Guiding Roberta by her arm, Mrs. Horvick deposited her at her desk where she collapsed, still sobbing and choking. A white imprint of Mrs. Horvick's hand stood out on her arm.

"Children, you will be quiet while Miss Barker and I have a short conference!" Mrs. Horvick shrilled at us. Miss Barker's face was white and she held her arms tightly against her body as she moved toward the door.

No one moved. I was afraid to move. I was afraid that what happened to Roberta would happen to me. I was afraid to look at Roberta. I don't remember the rest of the afternoon. The next day Roberta didn't come to school. In fact she never came again. Miss Barker told us Roberta's father decided to transfer her to the Rocky Boy school at the reservation.

I never saw Roberta again. I sometimes wonder what she learned from that experience. It's taken me years to understand what I learned.

You see, I loved Roberta. She was different. She was brown. She could run faster and jump higher than anyone else. She preferred being outside and she appeared smaller when she went indoors. She was connected to the earth. She was shy and afraid to read out loud. She talked in a soft voice. But most of all, she was different.

Roberta was different and somewhere inside I knew I was as different as she was. Only my differences didn't show. I learned when I was six and a half years old that I must never let others know how different I was. I learned to be different was not okay. And since being different was not okay, I had to be someone else. It's taken me 32 years to figure out, accept and love my differences. It's taken me 32 years to understand that my differences are part of my song. I wonder how Roberta is?

I believe that many of us have lost our songs. As children we were frightened by our experiences of the Mrs. Horvicks of the world and to survive we sacrificed ourselves. The greatest childhood wound of all is not to have been loved for what one truly was. The greatest adult wound is not to love yourself for who you truly are.

Long ago when we were children many of us discovered we lived in a world which threatened our well being. Most of us developed protective responses which helped us survive. These protective responses served us well as children, but as adults, each of us can benefit from uncovering our Original Map.

As children grow to adulthood, they will have a range of new experiences which will be viewed from the heart of this Original Map. Although most adults think they are acting freely, their present responses probably are influenced by their Original Map.

By the time an individual reaches adulthood, the Original Map operates without his conscious awareness. For the rest of my life, years after I had forgotten the incident with Mrs. Horvick, I was uncomfortable in new educational situations. It wasn't until I looked at my first experiences with the educational system that I had an idea of where the feelings of discomfort came from.

The Original Map must be uncovered, the experiences grieved and the map disassembled for the inner life journey to continue. Developing real time awareness of how past experiences are motivating us, allows us freedom to be who we are in the moment. When the Original Map is disassembled, then we are truly free to experience the reality of the moment.

The journey ends at Real Self. Real Self is the natural intuitive self who lives at the center of your being and speaks with a steady confident voice. It is living an authentic, truthful life connected to the natural order of who you are. People who live authentically are free to act because they are aware of their Original Map, their present patterns of behavior, what they believe and who they are. People who have claimed their Real Self are not swayed by the clamor of experts or media hype. They are people who honor themselves and their best work and continue to grow and develop as human beings. These people understand that claiming your Real Self does not mean you are free to do what you want without responsibility. On the contrary, claiming your Real Self means you accept 100% responsibility for your thoughts and actions. Discipline, clarity, simplicity and mindfulness are the tools for living Real Self.

If you choose to take this inner journey, sooner or later, you will have to face your own dragons, the fears that motivate your life. Only by facing these fears will you be free. Everyone has fears but to progress along the inner journey each person must learn to face the fears and walk through them. I mention the dragons right up front in this first chapter because I think it is important you understand the intensity of this inner journey. But, this probably isn't new information to you. Most of us have heard fairy tales about facing dragons since we were children. The fairy tales spoke to us symbolically, whispering of heros and dragons and the courage it would take to face life. As a child, I knew fairy tales conveyed an important message. It wasn't until I was an adult that I realized the fairy tales told of the inner journey each of us would have the opportunity to take in order to find ourselves. I use the word opportunity because the journey is a choice. Each person has the right to say "I will go no further" or "I choose not to grow." You may know people who have made the choice not to walk their own inner journey. Because everyone who travels this path will have to face their deepest fears, the inner journey takes courage.

The process of coming to awareness and integration is a journey of courage because each of us must find the courage to face ourselves. The first step in this journey is to reconstruct the Original Map of the world. Our first experiences in this life gave us the map for our human experience. But our first maps are frequently wrong or missing entire continents.

The first maps of earth were made from the accounts of sailors when they returned from their voyages. Most sailors protected their maps and kept them hidden because they believed to share them would give others an advantage. But one small country had a king who rewarded sailors who shared their maps. This small country had the most accurate maps in the world. Each time a sailor found a new river or a new land mass and reported it, he was rewarded. The king, in turn, shared all the information with his other sailors so that they could rely more and more on the accuracy of their maps.

For many people, their original childhood experiences are the maps of human experience from which they respond in daily life. This leaves many of us operating from inaccurate maps of what we have to do to get our needs met. Through the past years, I have shared my map of the life journey and I have been privileged that other "life sailors" have shared their maps with me. This book is written so that we can share our maps and get a deeper understanding of the journey.

2

Asking the Questions

"Who can say more than this rich praise, that
you alone are you."

Shakespeare

For 2,000 years people have been trying to understand the inner journey and what causes individuals to behave the way they do. Many philosophers believe all human beings are motivated to express their individual capacities and grow toward self integration. I believe that we have a deep desire to answer the question: "Who am I?" Intuitively humans know they must understand themselves to live authentic, creative, fulfilled lives.

Figure 2 has the question "Who am I?" in the center of three concentric circles. The answer to this question is central in the inner life journey to Real Self. The answer to "Who am I?" unfolds as the individual reaches greater awareness about her needs, beliefs, fears, past history and much more. Many people have limited awareness of how their past experiences influence their present day behaviors or how their natural fears motivate them to continue doing exactly what they are doing, even though it causes them pain. It is true that most people are internally motivated to be doing exactly what they are doing.

The questions in the two outer concentric circles are: "What should I do?" and "How should I interact?" These questions are related to "tasks" and "relationships" which are areas outside the inner self. The "Who am I?" question relates

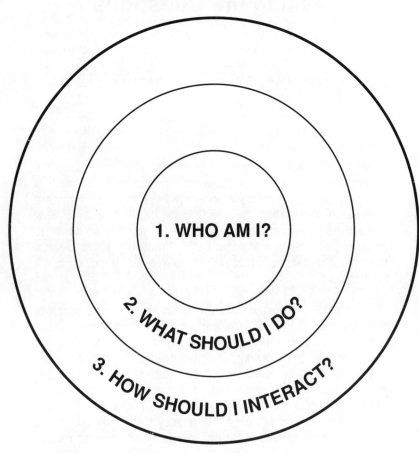

Figure 2

to the individual's communication with her inner self. The two questions: "What should I do?" and "How should I interact?" are focused outward toward responding to situations and people.

Much of the information we receive as we grow and develop is about the two outer circles; information such as how to get along with others, be a team player, manage time, influence others, get results, manage people, get good grades, sell product, etc. The answers to these outer focused questions are important, but the first question must be answered if the individual is ever to come home to Real Self.

For example, imagine a young man in college. His father and mother want only the best for him. They know how intelligent he is and they are encouraging him to be a doctor. In his second year of college, he is asked to declare a major or his intended area of study. He feels totally confused. He knows he likes the outdoors. He understands he has to earn money to get his food, clothing and shelter needs met. He is very aware that becoming a doctor would please his parents. If we looked into his past history, we would find a child whose Original Map has a statement like this: "When I please my parents, I feel loved. When I do not please my parents, I do not feel loved." As this young man wrestles with the outer two questions, he will not be able to come up with a satisfactory answer. His internal thinking might sound like this:

"What should I do? To please my parents, I should declare a Pre-med degree program. But I don't know if I want to be a doctor. I suppose I could try the Pre-med program and see if I like it. But, I know I really don't like being with sick people. Well, I suppose I could be a research doctor, then I could please my parents and not have to deal with people. But what if I get into it and find I don't like it. Then I'd really disappoint my parents because by then they'd expect me to be a doctor. They'd have told everyone that I was in the Pre-med program and then they'd be embarrassed because they'd have to explain that I'd changed majors. I'd end up looking wishy-washy and irresponsible and that would really make my Father angry. Maybe I should just talk to my parents. If I do that I better think about how I should interact. I don't want my father to get off on his agenda about how he hopes I am appreciating all the money this is costing him. Maybe I can say I want to get a degree in something like biology or math. Or, I could explain that after I graduate, I'd have a better idea of whether or not I want to be a doctor. Then I could still go on to medical school if I wanted to. Or maybe if I just told them I wasn't sure I wanted to spend all the time in college. No, that wouldn't work. Then they might start questioning what I was doing with my time. Hmmm, what should I do?"

The internal dialogue can go on indefinitely. He will not be able to answer the questions, "What should I do?" and "How should I interact?" to his satisfaction until he knows at least part of his answer to the question "Who am I?"

This type of internal dialogue can be generated whenever someone is unsure of a life choice such as whether or not to accept a promotion or move to a new location or change careers or get married or join an organization, etc. Like the young college student, many people will never be satisfied with their answers to the outer focused questions until they at least begin to answer the first question. For an authentic answer to the second and third question, "Who am I?" must be answered first. True satisfaction can never be found by looking outside of yourself. The life process of focusing on the "Who am I?" question gradually brings people to the realization that when they truly understand, accept and esteem themselves, nothing will be lacking in their lives. They will be free to celebrate themselves.

Ultimately all human growth is concerned with the freedom of the human spirit. Yet, people do not have the freedom to make aware life choices until they understand what causes them to behave the way they do. Each of us has a very detailed inner map of how to behave. This detailed inner map arises out of our personal history, our needs and our values. Each of us gains our inner self map in similar ways.

The journey begins with the "Original Self," who interacts with parents, siblings, grandparents, etc. and the physical environment: wet diapers, furry dogs, hot stoves, etc. The child is totally dependent on the world around her to meet her needs. Out of these original experiences of childhood, the child creates her first map of the world by interpreting her life experiences.

Most children cast themselves into the central role. For example, if her mother and father argue, she interprets their behavior as a sign that she is not being good enough. In fact, recent studies of children of divorce reveal that many children believe it's their fault that their parents' relationship failed.

From this first map of the world we build the patterns of our behavior. It's as if the first map projects the childhood experiences upon all other life experiences. The Original Map becomes a filter for all new experiences. This Original Map becomes very important because it is the only way we know how to survive in the world. Protecting the Original Map becomes paramount to survival. So, each new adult experience is filtered through this Original Map and is layered on top of the childhood experiences that form our life patterns.

Sam is a good example of how the Original Map filters adult life experiences. When he was born his parents' relationship was already in trouble. His presence and how to raise him became part of the on-going power struggle in his parents' relationship. Then one day, when he was three, his father divorced his mother and Sam became the weapon they could hurt each other with. He translated these experiences to mean: "I'm not good enough. If I were good enough my parents' relationship would be good. It's my fault my father left. Because I am bad, I can't trust people to meet my needs." Now that Sam is an adult he is very uncomfortable when people are kind and generous to him. It doesn't fit with his Original Map. Therefore, he filters and translates these experiences as: "People who do nice things for me must want something from me. I should be watchful of them."

The child's Original Map becomes the basis for determining her responses to the world. The stronger the childhood experience the more effort it will take to retranslate the Original Map. From the foundation of this Original Map, the adult creates specific behaviors that allow her to get her needs and values met. As the adult builds more and more complex behavioral patterns, she will probably have limited awareness of the role her Original Map plays in her day to day life.

Part of the inner journey is to dig through the patterns of behavior until the Original Map is reached. The adult has the capacity to retranslate the child's first experiences. The child may have experienced parents who didn't love her and translated this as: "If my own mother and father don't love me, I must be horrible." The adult has the ability to retranslate the childhood experience as: "My mother and father didn't have the capacity to love me. I was lovable. I was not horrible. I am lovable."

This inner journey takes courage because each individual must face her own worst fears. These fears are our personal dragons. They are the hidden fears such as: "I am unlovable." "I'm not worthy." "If people really knew me they'd think I'm a horrible person."

If the Original Map projects major dysfunctional behaviors, the adult is frequently forced to seek out counselors or therapists who will lead the adult through a process of uncovering why she behaves the way she does. Even more adults do not seek out counseling because they function well in our society, (i.e., hold jobs, obey the laws, maintain relationships). Yet, they still experience lives of quiet desperation because they feel powerless within their own lives and, at some level, they know that they are repeating life patterns which bring them negative consequences.

Until each individual faces these fears and retranslates the Original Map, the individual will not be able to make free, aware choices. Instead the adult will continually make the choices that comply with her Original Map view of the world.

Since Charlie has never uncovered his Original Map, he still operates from his first terrifying view of the world: "There was never enough. There was never enough to eat. There was never enough money. There was never enough!" Charlie's childhood experiences taught him that he'd never have enough money. So when he won a $250,000.00 lottery his first comment was: "It's not much... by the time I pay the taxes and make a few payments it'll be gone. You know money doesn't ever last very long. It doesn't matter how much I have, it's never enough." Regardless of what happens to Charlie he continues to view the world from his childhood experiences of never having enough money. Unless he retranslates his Original Map to match the current reality, he will continually be dissatisfied and unfulfilled about the state of his economic conditions.

Many people get caught in the patterns of their lives. They spend incredible amounts of time trying to understand the present situation without discovering how the past controls the present. People often replay the same situations in their lives, continually blaming others for their negative outcomes. If any situation has happened to you more than once it's probably part of YOUR PATTERN of behavior. If a situation has happened to you three or more times, it's a good chance that you are playing out your Original Map with different partners and in different environments.

Sara was having trouble with her boss. She believed her boss was sabotaging her work by giving her low performance ratings. After much searching Sara found another position which paid even better than her previous one. Sara was delighted for the first few months, then she perceived a co-worker started sabotaging her work.

Sara determined that part of her early childhood experiences involved a mother who was jealous of Sara's relationship with her father. Her mother subtly sabotaged Sara in her relationship with her father. Normal situations which involved disagreements looked like sabotage to Sara because she was projecting her Original Map of the world onto the situation.

Glen always had trouble with his employers valuing his work. He would work extremely hard, staying late and making sure everything was right, but he rarely got credit for his efforts. Instead his employers would point out the mistakes.

Nothing that Glen did was ever enough when he was a child. When his employers tell Glen, matter of factly, that they like his work, he doesn't hear them. He does however hear the one person's comment about the typo on page three of his report. In addition, Glen asks for raises even though he knows no one in the corporation has gotten a raise in the last year. Glen views this situation from his Original Map; he continually finds "facts" that prove his employers devalue his contributions.

These examples point out how the Original Map projects the child's translation of her experience into her adult life. Its almost as if a child grew up in Ireland then, as an adult, moved to a city in America. Yet, she still uses the map from Ireland to try to find streets in the American city. Of course she feels lost!

These examples seem very simple. The patterns are obvious. It's true that other people's patterns often seem obvious. Because these examples come from other people, it's easy to track the patterns. But, to the individual living in the patterns projected by the Original Map, the patterns are never obvious. For this individual, it is easy to blame the situation, other people, or even her horoscope. As long as the focus is outside of herself, there will never be an end to the blaming.

The following questions ask about the patterns of your life. Count the number of "yes's".

1. Do you have a distrust of yourself or of your capabilities?

2. Do you generally distrust others?

3. Are you surprised when people fulfill their agreements with you?

4. Do you distrust God?

5. Do you distrust nature?

6. Are you uncomfortable when you are alone for a long period of time?

7. Do you sometimes miss the signals when your body is hungry?

8. Are you unaware of how tired you are until it overwhelms you?

9. Do you often neglect your body needs?

10. Do you forget to eat?

11. Do you frequently cut down on your sleep?

12. Do you often feel that you never fit in?

13. Do you sense something is missing in your life?

Any "yes" response could be an indicator of unresolved past experiences which are part of your Original Map. A "yes" response is merely an indicator of an area for further exploration. Some people are so trapped in living the patterns projected from their Original Map, they cannot tell what a truthful answer is. They are so tangled up in the patterns, they cannot hear their truthful answers which come from the center of their being. All they know is they feel something missing. And when they are alone, or silent, they feel the pain of what is missing.

For most of us it is incredibly hard to even get a sense of our Original Maps. Since most of us operate from the Original Map, it is very difficult to find a "viewing point" that is not part of the Original Map. To make matters worse, we don't even have a language for talking about all this! In order to talk about this, I had to make up words such as Original Map and Real Self.

A language to talk about the life journey is critical. We must have words to describe what is happening to us so that we can communicate with ourselves and develop an internal dialogue that enables us make sense of our lives. When we don't have words to describe "who we are" or "what we need and value," the result is that we feel isolated and mute about our experiences and our lives.

Language shapes our world. The Eskimos have approximately fifty words for snow. Their language allows them to identify and share their experiences about the different kinds of snow. Americans have numerous words for money. They have a language for speaking about different kinds of money such as "interest," which is money made from investing money. We need a language that allows human beings to speak about their experiences, their needs, their beliefs and their differences.

While working as a consultant to Carlson Learning Company, I realized they have the copyright to a very insightful language. With their permission, I offer you the language of needs and values. Armed with this information, you have the language to communicate with yourself and others about the complexities of the life journey. All you have to bring with you is your courage.

The Carlson Learning Company uses a behavioral language which allows people to identify and describe their behaviors. They call their language NEEDS and VALUES. A need is anything we must have to live such as: food, clothing, shelter, safety, love, etc. A value is a belief. Needs-driven behaviors are instinctual or natural. Values-driven behaviors are thinking behaviors or "what we believe we should do."

To meet their needs people use a variety of behaviors: Dominance behaviors focus on overcoming and controlling both events and people, Influence behaviors focus on controlling people through interacting, Steadiness behaviors focus on maintaining the situation through cooperation with others, and Cautious behaviors focus on conserving the standards by doing things right. The behaviors we use to get our needs met are part of who we are.

Values are initially programmed by our parents and the culture we live in. By understanding our initial values and our original needs-driven behaviors, we can unravel the behavioral patterns and uncover the Original Map.

3

A Language to Honor our Differences

"The difference between the right word and the almost right word is the difference between lightning and lightning bug."

Mark Twain

I enjoy quiet evenings which sometimes include close friends and often include a good book. I have friends who enjoy parties which include dozens of people and loud music. In the beginning I went to the parties and wondered what was wrong with me when I didn't enjoy myself. I thought surely something must be wrong with me because so many others seemed to enjoy what I didn't. For years I tried to figure out how to explain to my more extroverted friends that I really didn't want to attend their festivities. But, it wasn't until I found a language to clearly and respectfully explain our differences that we were able to come to terms with each other's different needs. Now my friends, who enjoy their enthusiastic parties, still invite me and often I decline with their best wishes. Sometimes I go for a short time. And for that short interval, I enjoy our differences but I know I won't stay long because my song comes to me in silence.

Whoever you are and whatever you need, you can more easily tell your story when you can speak a language that explains and honors your differences. Even as children these differences are recognizable. Parents often recognize these differences early in their children's lives with statements like these:

"She was always active; even as a baby she couldn't sit still."

"He's was always such a good, quiet child. He never gave me a bit of trouble."

"He's always been talkative."

"His report cards always had a comment from his teacher about how his talking disrupted the class."

"We have two children. One likes to spend time alone in her room. Her sister thinks being alone is punishment."

Like adults, children use different behaviors to get their needs met. Every one has needs: food, clothing, shelter, love, belonging and self-actualization. How these needs are met is critical in the development of healthy self esteem.

Each person has a natural behavioral style that he will use to try to get his needs met. A child usually has not developed the discernment to use appropriate behaviors situationally. Although everyone's natural behaviors have clear strengths, most parents have first hand evidence of the weaknesses of their child's behavioral style.

By using the language of behaviors to explain those first experiences as a child, people can gain information about past behaviors which may influence who they are today. By understanding these past natural behaviors, individuals can gain a clearer understanding of their Original Map, retranslate some of their first experiences and began to accept and esteem their past natural behaviors.

There are four behavioral categories or styles which people tend to use to get their needs met. They are Dominance, Interaction, Steadiness and Cautious. No one style is better than another. They are just different ways of behaving. Each style has strengths and weaknesses.

A Dominant child, operating out of his strengths, is decisive and results oriented. This same child operating out of his behavioral weaknesses may seem demanding and belligerent. An Interacting child has high verbal ability as a strength. To her parents, who are around her daily, she may seem to chatter incessantly. A Steadiness child's easy-going style may appear to be passive and a Cautious child's attention to doing everything correctly may appear to be perfectionistic.

Parents are often baffled by the range of behavioral differences in siblings. In fact many parents are dismayed to discover that their children do not have the same behavioral preferences of either parent. The parents who naturally enjoy quiet time without activity may be surprised to find their son wants to be active all of his waking hours. Parents who naturally want to be more involved with people may be surprised to discover their child likes playing quietly alone. Every parent has to determine how to provide healthy self esteem to a child who has behaviors which are clearly different from their own and often, when the child is operating from his behavioral weaknesses, unacceptable.

Ideally children need to be esteemed for their natural behaviors. In reality most children experience a range of criticism for their natural behaviors; criticism which varies from "putdowns" to abuse.

Putdowns can be direct or masquerade as humor. In fact, parents frequently tease their children about their behavioral characteristics by saying things like: "We call her motor mouth because she never stops talking."

There is a good possibility that many children's first life experiences occur with parents who are totally baffled by their children's natural behaviors. Since most children are seen from their weaknesses, parents may perceive the child's natural behavior as NOT okay. This should be no surprise, since most people judge behaviors like their own as okay and behaviors unlike theirs as NOT okay. A child who does not share his parents natural behavioral preferences may be told in various ways that he should be different. Please note that the parent is not saying the child's behaviors need to be more effective. The parent is in fact saying; "I want you to be different." Most parents do not intend to send a "don't be who you are" message, but they may be at their wits end raising a child whose behaviors are, at the least, puzzling and at most, terribly frustrating.

Often, through parental words and actions or through the child's interpretation of events, the child receives a "you should be different than you are message." This type of message tells a child "not to be who he is." To get his needs met he gives up his natural behavior. It is this natural behavior that the child may perceive is judged as wrong and, since this natural behavior is part of the child's natural energy state, the child comes to experience himself as wrong. The child's experience of being wrong, becomes part of his Original Map.

As the child grows, the behavioral differences become even clearer. By the time Mary was in sixth grade, her differences were painfully obvious to her mother. Mary was a quiet, easy-going child who preferred to have only one or two close friends. Mary's mother was popular and outgoing with literally hundreds of friends and acquaintances. Mary's mother wanted Mary to experience the "good things," such as being voted cheerleader. Mary's mother wanted this for the good of her daughter and she believed good social skills were critical for success in life. She expected Mary to have a wide range of friends. Mary's teachers told her mother that Mary was quiet and shy in class. Mary's mother continually said: "Mary, why are you so quiet and shy? I don't know where you get it? You're not like me or your father. You should speak up in class. You should find more friends." The message Mary heard and translated to her Original Map, which was to project itself into her adult life, was "Being quiet and shy is NOT okay. To be okay, you must be different. You should be different than you are. To succeed in life you must be someone else."

It is important to point out that Mary's mother wasn't trying purposely to sabotage or lower her daughter's self esteem. Mary's mother wanted only the best for her child. Regardless of the intent, Mary grew up hearing the message: "You can't be who you are."

When I met Mary she was still behaving as a talkative, animated, enthusiastic person.   When she discovered that there was a quiet, reserved, natural energy residing within her, she was relieved. When she accepted that this energy was all right, even wonderful, she cried. Then she retranslated her Original Map and reclaimed part of herself. She wrote: "My mother wanted me to be like her. I am not like my mother. I am myself. I have a naturally quiet and reserved energy which I love. I don't have to be different to be loved. I am okay as I am." The behavioral changes in Mary were immediately evident. She was more relaxed, she talked less, she was less tired. Her co-workers asked her what was wrong? Mary answered, "I am more at peace with myself."

Brandon is a naturally talkative child. He makes friends easily. In fact, he knows everyone on the block where he lives. His parents are sometimes overwhelmed by 6 year old Brandon's ability to control conversations; even with other adults. Brandon's father was careful to reinforce this message: "You are okay. You are naturally talkative and that's good." In addition, Brandon's father redirected some of his son's natural tendencies by saying: "People like you, who are naturally talkative, must be sure that everyone gets a chance to speak, so sometimes you must listen."

In this case Brandon is esteemed for his natural behaviors while cautioned about the needs of others. Since Brandon is still 6 years old we don't know how he is translating this message to his Original Map. He may be hearing: "I'm really an okay person and one of the best parts of me is that I can talk!" or he may be hearing: "I'm not okay because I don't listen enough."

The examples of Mary and Brandon reveal natural behaviors. Brandon was naturally "Interactive" or focused on the people around him. Mary's more natural behavior was quiet and easy-going or the "Steadiness" behavior, yet for much of her life she believed that she should act like an Interactive person to be okay.

The amazing truth about the life journey is that there will never be any perfect parents. AND even if there was the possibility of having perfect parents, each child would still translate his experiences from his "child viewpoint". The Original Map is the map of a child's view. Each individual has to discover and retranslate his Original Map to reflect current reality or he will never reach the self actualizing state of Real Self.

It's important to understand that as a child, you were naturally motivated by your own needs-driven behavior. All children are motivated for their own reasons, NOT for their parents' reasons. By understanding the natural behaviors of who they were as children, adults can move toward understanding their first experiences and begin to create an environment to retranslate their Original Map

The following check list can be used to gain more information about your Original Map. Think about who you were in grade school. Then check the behaviors you remember exhibiting. Adults frequently say "I'll never remember that far back." Yet, when they take their time and remember one of their grade school teachers or a significant situation from their grade school years they do get a fairly accurate picture of "how they experienced their childhood years."

BEHAVIORAL CHECKLIST[1]

Check those behaviors which you exhibited in grade school.

BEHAVIORAL CATEGORY I

___As a child, I preferred to communicate directly, quickly and to "tell" what I wanted.

---

1. For a more accurate assessment of your past behavior, you will want to take the Personal Development Profile as you think about your grade school behavior. The Personal Development Profile is available from Carlson Learning Company. More information is in the Resource Section on page 103.

___As a child, I acted forcefully and boldly.

___As a child, I could usually hold my own ground with children my own age and even with some adults.

___As a child, I was willing to take risks.

___As a child, I was less dependent on help and often preferred to do things myself.

BEHAVIORAL CATEGORY II

___As a child, I acted enthusiastically in most situations.

___As a child, I acted spontaneously and carefree.

___As a child, I found others interesting and I liked to be with people.

___As a child, I acted in an outgoing manner and I met people easily.

___As a child, I may have been sentimental or had emotional highs and lows.

BEHAVIORAL CATEGORY III

___As a child, I acted patiently in most situations.

___ As a child, I usually listened more than I talked.

___As a child, I tended to be cooperative and my parents frequently were impressed by "what a good child" I was.

___As a child, I was seen as easy-going.

___As a child, I was less active toward trying new things and usually preferred the old or familiar.

BEHAVIORAL CATEGORY IV

___As a child, I was usually conscientious.

___As a child, I was cautious in most situations.

___As a child, I liked to think things through.

___As a child, I liked privacy and may not have shared my thoughts.

___As a child, I was usually diplomatic.

Count up the number of checks you made in each category. Determine which two categories have the most checks. Then read the descriptions of children from those two categories.

BEHAVIORAL CATEGORY I: ACTIVE AND DECISIVE

Children with this Dominant behavioral style hate to lose. They may be somewhat demanding. They may ask a lot of questions. They may want to control the environment by "being the boss." Often they "tell" instead of ask. And, they are not afraid to barge in. These children are not afraid to fight for what they need or want. These children can be identified by their drive to get tasks done quickly. In the classroom, these children may have trouble sitting for long periods of time. They have a natural energy that begs for activity. They need to take some type of action. If they are forced to sit still for long periods of time they may resort to "stirring up" trouble.

BEHAVIORAL CATEGORY II: TALKATIVE AND ANIMATED

Children with this Interactive behavioral style may like to show off or be the center of attention. They are able to get most people to listen to them talk. They usually make friends very easily and they can be quite charming. They tend to want popularity and may be able to butter up others to get what they want. They know how to get attention and can easily talk to almost anyone, even groups. You can identify children with this behavioral style by their drive to talk or interact with all types of people. The most frequent comments you'll find on these children's report cards are: "Her talking frequently disrupts the class. If Susan would learn to do her own work instead of discussing it with others she would receive higher marks." "Jack always volunteers to answer questions." "Pat is good at contributing to the classroom discussions."

BEHAVIORAL CATEGORY III: SOFT SPOKEN AND COOPERATIVE

Children with this Steadiness behavioral style probably dislike fighting. They prefer to cooperate with others. They tend to come across as soft spoken and quiet. They usually try hard to see the good in people and they tend to take pride in being pleasant to others. These children like things and people to stay just the way they are. They prefer to listen and may try to prove "just how nice they can be." These children may allow other children to get the attention. They do not have to be the star, but they do like sincere recognition. On their report cards these children are frequently commended because of their ability to get along with other children and be part of a team. You can identify these children by how well they listen, by how well they cooperate with other children and by their relaxed, easy-going energy.

BEHAVIORAL CATEGORY IV: CAUTIOUS AND CONCERNED ABOUT DOING THINGS CORRECTLY

Children with this Cautious behavioral style like to do things correctly. They like to plan ahead and know what the rules are. They prefer to know the exact answers. Usually they keep their rooms organized and neat. They usually like to have time to think before deciding anything. They may sometimes fret and worry. They probably are very careful of key details such as how they take care of their favorite toys.

They may ask probing questions which seem too adult for them. You can identify these children by how carefully they do their tasks, by how well they follow the rules and by the nature of their questions, which may seem somewhat critical or judgmental.

As you read through the descriptions it is very important that you do not label your natural behaviors as good or bad. There is no best behavioral style or category. Humans have natural behaviors which they use to get their needs met. This language describes those natural behaviors. Many people have a judgmental reaction to their own natural behavior; "My behavior is best." Some people react to the behavioral style of others; "There must be one best way to act. Since we are different, their behavior must be wrong." Remember, there is no one best behavioral style or way to act.

Please do not use this language to judge others as wrong or not okay. As humans we do this enough already. The whole world, from plastic surgeons to fashion consultants, appears to tell us how "wrong" we are. This language is meant to offer you a new language for understanding and accepting yourself. With this language you can communicate with yourself and others. As humans we need a language that allows us to explain "who we are," a language that offers us ways to become more effective in our lives, ways to accept ourselves and others and new ways of understanding how our behavior affects our lives and the lives of others. It is critically important to use this language to understand the natural differences that occur in human behavior. This language is a tool to nurture and honor your natural behaviors.

4

The Inner Child

"We all have a child within us. We may return to these deeply ingrained child behaviors when we are in unfavorable situations. In addition, the inner child may continually act in ways to get his or her past unmet needs satisfied. Understanding, accepting and dealing with your internal, past child is a method of increasing your present day effectiveness."

Classical Styles Audio Album

Who were you as a child? How did you perceive the world? How did you interpret your world? What does your Original Map look like?

By answering these types of questions and by understanding your behavior as a child, you can develop a deeper understanding of yourself and gain insights into why you behave the way you do today. Bradshaw in his book, *Bradshaw: On The Family*, says that "Until we contact the vital spontaneous natural child who was abandoned ... we cannot begin to restore our inner life. We have to go back and contact our lost self if we are to discover our true self."

More and more professionals in human behavior are accepting that childhood experiences contained within adults still influence their present day thoughts, desires, and beliefs. This is especially true when the adult is in a negative situation.

In unfavorable situations the fear-driven behavior of the inner child may be triggered. The result is that when you are under pressure you may feel like a small rageful child living in an adult body while others may be stunned at your reactions.

To understand your natural reactions which arise from your Original Map, it is important to understand the behavioral fears and goals you had as a child. If you were a Dominant child you were active. Your childhood behavioral goal was to direct or control your environment so that you could get what you needed. You were able to make fast decisions about what you wanted and you were probably "direct" in your communications. You may have wanted freedom from parental supervision and you probably liked new and varied activities. Parents or teachers may have labeled you as "willful" or "demanding" in response to your naturally more closed point of view.

If you were a Dominant child yesterday, then today, when you find yourself in stressful situations you may become impatient, fearful of being taken advantage of or reactive to personal criticism. These stressful situations may occur when you perceive you are losing, you are personally under attack or others are telling you what to do. At these times you may experience emotional responses which are out of proportion to the actual situation; a critical signal that your inner child energy is responding.

If you were an Interactive child, you were active and people oriented. Your childhood behavioral goal was to relate positively with others, allowing you to interact with others so you could get what you needed. You were probably enthusiastic and animated in your communications. Your teachers may have labeled you as "talkative" and "friendly" in response to your more open point of view

If you were an Interactive child yesterday, then today, in stressful situations, you may find yourself becoming disorganized, fearful of people's disapproval of you or afraid of personal rejection. These stressful situations may occur when you perceive that others dislike you, reject your friendliness or want to argue or fight. At these times you may experience an emotional reaction such as tears or outbursts. These outbursts may be out of proportion to the actual situation signalling your return to the needs-driven behavior of your inner child.

If you were a child with a Steadiness behavioral style, you were easy-going and cooperative with others. Your childhood behavioral goal was to take actions and make choices that would maintain stability in your life. You may have been most comfortable in situations which were predictable and stable. Your teachers may have labeled you as a "good worker" or a "team player" in response to your cooperative, open point of view.

If you had a Steadiness behavioral pattern as a child, then today in stressful situations you may find yourself: avoiding risks, resisting change, or being overprotective of your work, your family, your friends, your security, etc. These stressful situations may occur when you perceive: you don't understand what's happening, others are competing with you, or there are unexpected changes. At these times you may experience a reaction which could be either an emotional withdrawal from the situation or an emotional outburst. Both of these reactions could be out of proportion to the actual situation signalling that you are responding to the needs of your inner child.

If you were a Cautious child, you were reserved in expression and attentive to what others said. You rarely interrupted anyone. Your privacy was important to you and you responded cautiously to new people and situations. Your childhood behavioral goal was to do things the correct way. Your teachers may have labeled you as "conscientious" with your work or as "perfectionist" in response to the amount of attention you paid to your work and the rules.

If you had a Cautious behavioral pattern as a child, then today, in stressful situations, you may find yourself becoming overly critical, afraid of making errors in your work, or sensitive to criticism about your ideas or your work. These stressful situations may occur when you perceive: others are criticizing your work or your efforts, others are asking blunt or invasive questions about your work or when you are involved in a situation where the information is incomplete or inaccurate.

An effective strategy for integrating your past child with your present day awareness involves an internal process. First you will want to re-establish contact with your own past. In order to re-establish contact with your past, you must create a safe place within yourself. No where is there a place more tranquil or safe for your past child than the place you create within yourself. To create this safe place follow these steps.

Find a quiet environment where you will not be disturbed. Remain seated in an upright, yet comfortable position. Do not cross your legs or arms. Sit so that your spine is naturally straight and your head is balanced comfortably on your neck. You may want to rotate your neck slightly from side to side and from front to back until you find the balance point. The balance point for your neck is the place where it doesn't take any muscle effort to hold your head in a naturally upright, but not rigid, position. Spend as much time as you want finding the right position so that you feel physically comfortable, yet alert. The first time you attempt this you may find that you spend all your time finding your comfortable position. The important point is not to proceed with the next step until you feel physically comfortable, alert, and relaxed. This step allows you to quiet your body.

After you have discovered your comfortable position focus your attention on your breathing. You may notice your breath as the air moves in and out of your nostrils or you might simply focus your attention on the rising and falling of your abdomen. Take a deep breath and allow your body to relax. Then with each continuing breath allow your body to relax more and more. Do not try to control your breathing. Just let yourself breathe naturally. Keep your attention focused on your breathing. You may find that your thoughts begin to wander. When you notice your thoughts wandering just gently identify what's happening by saying to yourself "Quiet please." Then refocus your attention on your breathing. Do this for several minutes until your thoughts become more quiet and you are able to maintain your attention on your breathing. The first few times you attempt this, it's natural to spend most of your time noticing your thoughts and saying; "Quiet Please" and very little time maintaining your focus on your breathing. The important point is not to proceed until you feel your thoughts quiet down. This step allows you to quiet your mind.

After you have focused your attention on your breathing for a while, then allow yourself to create in your mind's eye a safe place for yourself. As you create this internal safe place be sure to use all your senses. What does this safe place look like? Some people create an image of a sandy beach and an ocean, others want their safe place to be in the mountains, still others feel safe in a deep quiet cavern that looks out upon a meadow. Be sure you choose what constitutes a safe place for you. Spend some time "seeing" this place in your mind's eye. Then answer the question, "What does it feel like?" Some people say they feel cool breezes blowing. Others experience the warm sun on their skin. Whatever you choose, be sure that the safe place you create has the right feeling for you. Spend some time in this safe place and bring your senses with you. Determine what you hear, taste, and smell in your safe place. The more senses you can bring to your safe place, the more you will be able to truly experience the tranquil, safe place within yourself. The important point about this step is that you are learning to find the center or quiet place within yourself from which you can develop greater awareness about yourself. From this tranquil, safe place within yourself you can learn to integrate yourself: your past energy, your present needs and your values.

After you have discovered your quiet place and have gone to this quiet place several times over a period of several days, then allow yourself to begin to reconnect with your past child energy. The day you choose to start reconnecting with your child energy you will want to follow all the steps. First quiet your body. Second, quiet your mind. Third, spend a few minutes relaxing in your quiet place.

From this safe place imagine yourself going back in time to the school you attended as a child. Then imagine a child standing in front of the school. The child is you. Imagine yourself going over to the child and bending down to talk to him or her. You must determine what to call your inner child. You may want to call your child by a special name, perhaps your favorite childhood nickname, but most certainly you will not want to use your adult name to speak to your inner child. Be gentle. Your inner child may be shy. It may take time for your own inner past child energy to learn to trust you. As you build trust in this relationship with yourself and your inner child, you will gain more trust in your abilities, your intuition, and in yourself.

This is not a one time process. The relationship that you are developing with your inner child must be an on-going relationship. As you continue to develop this relationship with yourself, you will be able to receive more information about your feelings, your fears, how your past influences you, and your needs. The internal child energy will be able to communicate with you in your own internal quiet space. Simply put: you are creating an internal place to communicate with yourself so that you can gather information from yourself, about yourself so that you can integrate yourself. You will want to practice what you say to your child. The following paragraphs will help you decide exactly what to say to your inner child during your first meeting.

If you identified yourself as having a Dominant style when you were a child, you will want to say: "I'm sorry that I haven't listened more closely to you before. What you need is very important to me. You don't have to change to be loved. I love you just as you are. I love you for who you are. I like your active energy. It's okay for you to tell me what you need. I'm glad you continually question what's happening to me. It's okay for you to remind me to think about what I need and what I believe. I'm sorry I was unable to take better care of your needs. I'll meet you in this quiet place to talk at least once a week." (Determine your own time schedule for checking with your inner child. You may plan to connect once a day, once a week or however often you want. But a word of warning; whatever you tell your inner child you will do, be sure to live up to it or you will learn that you cannot trust yourself).

If you identified your childhood style as Interacting, you will want to say: "I'm sorry that I haven't paid more attention to you before this. Your needs are important to me. You are loved for who you are. You don't have to change to be loved. I like your natural enthusiastic energy. I'm glad that you continually express yourself to me. I'm glad that you like to interact with others. It's okay to have fun. I like that you are playful. I'm sorry that I was unable to take better care of your needs. I'll meet you in this quiet place to talk at least once a week." (Determine your own time schedule for checking with your inner child. You may plan to connect once a day, once a week or however often you want. But a word of warning; whatever you tell your inner child you will do, be sure to live up to it or you will learn you cannot trust yourself).

If you identified your past child behavior as the Steadiness style, you will want to say: " I'm sorry that I haven't appreciated you before this. Your needs are important to me. You are loved for who you are. You don't have to change to be loved. I like your easy-going energy. I like the way you try to cooperate with others. I know how hard you try. I know how hard you work. I understand your kind and gentle nature. I'm sorry that I haven't taken better care of your needs. I'll meet you in this quiet place to talk with you at least once a week." (Determine your own time schedule for checking with your inner child energy. You may plan to connect once a day, once a week or however often you want. But a word of warning; whatever you tell your inner child you will do, be sure to live up to it or you will learn that you cannot trust yourself).

If you were a Cautious child, you will want to say: "I'm sorry that I haven't encouraged and honored you before this. Your needs are important to me. You are okay just as you are. You don't have to change to be loved. I like your thoughtful energy. I'm glad you are cautious. I like the way you are attentive to what others say. It's okay to take your time. It's okay to want to do things well. I'm sorry I was unable to take better care of your needs. I'll meet you in this quiet place to talk at least once a week." (Determine your own time schedule for checking with your inner child. You may plan to connect once a day, once a week or however often you want. But a word of warning; whatever you tell your inner child you will do, be sure to live up to it or you will learn that you cannot trust yourself).

It may take time to establish a connection with your inner child. Some people are able to imagine a picture of the child they were and then hold an internal dialogue with that image. Others can internally hear the conversation with themselves and their inner child by role playing the dialogue in their minds. Since everyone internally talks to him or herself, this type of "internal dialogue" is fairly common. Still others report a "feeling" almost like they are hugging their internal child and instead of dialogue they experience emotions. Whatever happens is part of the process of figuring out how to interact with yourself. Take time to get to know yourself and give yourself permission to be accepting, not judging of whatever happens.

A word of warning, STOP THIS PROCESS if you find yourself judging yourself by saying things like: "Oh, I didn't like that experience." "My inner child is a monster." "I don't like her." "I don't like him." Remember, the purpose of this process is to accept and embrace your inner child as a method of integrating your past energies. It will do you no good to judge the past child as bad or inadequate. Judging the inner child or the experience of meeting your inner child as "not enough" is one way you can distance or disintegrate yourself.

It may take a short or a long time to establish a connection with your past internal child energy. The child energy is usually experienced when adults feel under pressure and return to their childhood behavioral patterns. The key to integrating and making peace with this energy is to have an on-going relationship with yourself.

Plan time daily or weekly to quiet your body and your thoughts and relax in your safe place while you listen to hear if your internal child has anything to say. Several individuals reported that the first few times they followed this process, they were overwhelmed by the anger they experienced as their child-self complained. If you find your inner child complaining during the first few weeks, be patient and listen with compassion not judgement. You may have to apologize to your inner child. There is something incredibly powerful when the adult self says to the child self: "I'm so sorry that you didn't feel loved. I love you!" Assure your inner child that you are committed to a relationship and that you value the information you gain by listening to your inner voice.

In time you will be able to connect with your inner energy from your quiet place. Then you will be able to start to negotiate with your inner child about your "over reactions to certain types of stressful situations." But a word of caution, do not try to negotiate about stressful situations until you have established a trust, a comfort level and a connection with your inner child. When you experience a deep loving feeling for your inner child, then you will want to use the following paragraphs to negotiate.

If you were a child with a Dominant behavioral style, you will want to ask your inner child, "What makes him afraid?" Ask him to explain what happens when he senses that you are losing control or being taken advantage of or being personally criticized. He will probably explain how afraid or embarrassed he feels.

Most children with Dominant style behaviors react in fear-driven behavior when they perceive things are out of their control. Tell your inner child you understand how scary "not being in charge is." Ask your inner child to let you, the adult, manage the situation. Explain that the adult-you, has more ability to handle scary situations. Negotiate with your inner child. You probably will come to a point where your inner child agrees you can take over, but only if you promise him that you will take care of him. Taking care of your inner child means you must leave any situation if your child requests it. Practically this means in difficult situations you may have to say to the other adults involved "I am going to take a breather for a few minutes. I will be glad to discuss this difficult topic later." Later could be in a few minutes or tomorrow or next week. Either way you have maintained your agreement that you will leave situations if your inner child requests it. The commitments that you make to yourself and keep are critical if you are to trust, value and esteem yourself.

If you were an Interactive child, you will want to ask your inner child what he is afraid of and to explain how he feels when he perceives people are rejecting or disapproving of him. He will probably respond by telling you how afraid and abandoned he feels. Most children with Interactive behavioral styles react with fear-driven behaviors such as tears or emotional outbursts when they feel rejected or disapproved of. Tell your inner child you understand how frightening it is when it appears others are rejecting you. Ask your inner child if he is comfortable with allowing you, the adult, to deal with people who are disapproving. Explain that some people don't approve of anyone and that sometimes people may be angry at the situation and not actually rejecting you. Ask the inner child to inform you when he is feeling threatened so that you can take care of him. Practically this may mean you might have to say to your inner child: "Inner child's name, this is not about you. You are okay. The people here are angry about the situation. You are not being rejected." If the situation escalates, you must remove yourself before your inner child reacts in fear. As the adult you are responsible for watching your own internal tension and gently excusing yourself to take care of your needs BEFORE the situation explodes.

If you were a Steadiness child, you will want to ask your inner child what he is afraid of and to explain how he feels when he perceives his security is being threatened. Security may be physical, emotional, relationship, job, or even spiritual. Ask your inner child to explain what he experiences when unexpected changes occur and what happens when he is faced with risks. He will probably respond by telling you how afraid and unsafe he feels. Most children with Steadiness behavioral styles react with fear-driven behaviors such as withdrawal, or quiet stubbornness when they feel their security is threatened. Tell your inner child you understand how frightening it is when it appears his security is being threatened by unexpected change or when situations seem risky. Ask your inner child if he is comfortable with allowing you, the adult, to deal with situations that involve change, are perceived as risky or seem unsafe. Explain that the adult-you has the ability to keep the inner child safe. In situations which appear unsafe the adult-you can ask questions to clarify exactly what is happening. Sometimes the adult-you may determine that the risky situation will become more secure as time goes on. Let the inner child know that life is not always secure but you, the adult, have the ability to keep the inner child safe. Ask the child to inform you when he is feeling threatened so that you can take care of him. Practically this may mean you might have to say to your inner child: "Inner child's name, this situation does appear to be risky or unsafe. Please trust me to determine what is best for us. We may have to wait until things settle down to regain the sense of security. But you can be secure that I am watchful of what is happening and trying to do what is best for both of us." If the situation escalates to "highly unsafe," in the perception of your inner child, you must remove yourself before your inner child reacts in fear. As the adult, you are responsible for watching your own internal tension and gently excusing yourself to take care of your needs BEFORE you react in fear.

If you were a Cautious child, you will want to ask your inner child what he is afraid of and to explain how he feels when he perceives his work or ideas are being criticized. Ask your inner child to explain what he experiences when he makes mistakes and when things do not turn out the way he planned. He will probably respond by telling you how afraid he feels when his work doesn't live up to his expectations or standards. He may explain that he is terrified of making mistakes and he is critical of not only his work but also himself. He may expect himself to be perfect. Most children with Cautious behavioral styles react with fear-driven behaviors like indirect fighting or becoming overly critical. In addition, Cautious styles often worry and spend extraordinary amounts of time reacting to mistakes. Tell your inner child you understand how frightening it is when it appears others are criticizing his work or ideas. Assure your inner child that everyone makes mistakes from time to time and that fear of mistakes may prevent him from doing his best work. Ask your inner child if he is comfortable with allowing you, the adult, to handle people who are critical of your work or ideas. Explain that frequently, if you do not react to the implied criticism, you can have higher quality work by incorporating others' ideas. Remind your inner child of your commitment to the highest standard of work. Explain that you, the adult, have the ability to sort out the useful ideas from the criticism and keep the inner child safe. Remind the inner child that the adult-you can redirect others criticism by saying: "Please tell me what suggestions you have that will make the work better instead of telling me what you don't like." Let the inner child know that all human beings make mistakes and that you have the ability to handle your mistakes and keep the inner child safe. Ask the inner child to inform you when he is feeling threatened so you can take care of him. Practically this may mean you might have to say to your inner child: "Inner child's name, this person is being very critical. This criticism tells us more about the other person than about our work. Let's listen for any ideas we can use to make our work better without letting the criticism get to us. I am trying to do what is best for both of us." If the criticism escalates you must remove yourself before your inner child self reacts in fear. As the adult, you are responsible for watching your own internal tension and gently excusing yourself to take care of your needs BEFORE you react in fear. To the person who is criticizing you, you might say: "I will be happy to discuss this further at a later time. It would be best for me if I could see what you have to say in writing. Please, jot down your suggestions so I can look at them before we talk and I will be prepared to respond to your concerns." Then you must leave and NOT engage in further discussion or you risk an emotional reaction.

It's critically important to maintain your commitments to the inner child part of you. These are the commitments you make to yourself. Be cautious about making any commitments. Do NOT make commitments you cannot keep or you will learn to distrust yourself. It is better to say to your inner child: "I don't know if I can always leave situations when you request it. But, I promise to do my best to care for you during the event and to talk with you about how I can do better for us after the situation is over." A sincere commitment to an inner child involves listening, esteeming and maintaining promises.

Listen to your inner child, especially when he is feeling threatened. Physical responses such as: shallow breathing, queasy stomach, tight shoulders, etc. are clues that your inner child's needs-driven energy is not being cared for.

Take actions to esteem your inner child. By taking the time to speak with your inner child with a quiet body and mind, you are sending the message that you consider him an important part of you. By promising your inner child to respect his fears and keep him safe, you are sending yourself the message that you have worth, that you count, that you are important.

Maintain your promises with your inner child. If you consistently place the needs of others before your own inner child needs, you send the message that you are worth less than others. Under the guise of not being selfish, many people ignore their own needs. Remember, for any extended period of time, you cannot treat anyone else any better than you treat yourself. When you consistently break promises to your inner child, you can disintegrate your being to the point that you will not recognize when you break promises to others. What you do to yourself, you will do to others. For example, the parent who doesn't love himself will probably have difficulty loving his children.

Your inner child is more than just needy child energy which may have been ignored by you as an adult. This inner child energy or thought or whatever you want to call it, is your creative, playful, joyous part of your existence. By ignoring your inner child energy you slowly and painfully kill the creative, playful part of yourself.

5

Beliefs

Though words are not reality, they can verify our truth by describing our experience.

A philosopher once said "the unexamined life isn't worth living." Examining your life experiences means that you spend time thinking about who you are and how to live an authentic life. Your beliefs form an important part of who you are. Beliefs are the conclusions you have formed based on your life experiences. Your first experiences were with your parents or parental figures. So it makes sense that your first beliefs would come from these experiences. Part of your childhood experiences were with teachers and peer groups. These experiences also played a role in developing your beliefs. In addition, the culture you lived in helped form your first conclusions about "what was right". All of these past experiences together form the framework of your initial belief system.

To develop a deep understanding of the answer to "who am I?" an individual must clearly understand and act out of what she believes. She must honestly face her daily actions and hold them up to her beliefs to determine if she is living according to her own values.

To grasp the magnitude of your own belief system, you must think about your basic assumptions; what role you play in every experience, what you think is the right action for you to take, and what prevents you from living a life based on your beliefs. These questions are a beginning toward understanding how your beliefs influence your actions.

To uncover the beliefs which guide your life, you can use several approaches. Different approaches might include speaking with an expert on values, attending courses about ethics or using an instrument called the *Values Profile System.*[2] This instrument can help you identify your beliefs and categorize them into four values systems consisting of interrelated beliefs.

Another approach might involve spending time, weekly or monthly, examining and claiming your beliefs. Whatever approach you use, it is crucial to your inner life journey that you examine the beliefs which guide you. Your beliefs play a profound role in who you are.

One of the best ways to examine who you are in the light of your beliefs is by keeping a journal of your beliefs and experiences. I highly recommend using both, the *Values Profile System* and keeping a values journal.

To keep a values journal, you must be committed to the process of examining and claiming your beliefs. This commitment takes discipline. Discipline does not take a lot of time or energy. It does mean you live up to the promises you make. If you make a commitment with yourself for a weekly or monthly time to examine your beliefs, you must keep the appointment. You can choose a Saturday morning when everyone is in bed or an evening when others are involved elsewhere. The appointment doesn't have to be long. The first time you make an appointment with yourself you may want to commit to 15 or 20 minutes. Be sure to set up the parameters of the appointment so that you can be successful. Be gentle with yourself when you set up the schedule. Be firm with yourself when you keep your promises to yourself.

2. The Values Profile System offers a more accurate assessment of your belief systems. It is available from Carlson Learning Company. More information is in the Resource Section on page 103.

Don't schedule time for yourself when you know others have expectations of you. Don't schedule so much time you feel trapped. If you choose to schedule an appointment with yourself you must set it up so that you have a successful experience.

If you choose to make an appointment with yourself, please don't break it or you will send the message to yourself that you are not committed to your own life journey. It's better that you choose not to journal at all than to offer yourself another experience of not living up to commitments to yourself. If you choose to make an appointment with yourself and you keep it, you will gain one more experience of self trust. This is the trust which builds your relationship with yourself. These experiences teach you to love yourself.

In figure 1, the map on page 13, there is a bridge. It's called the Bridge of Choice. When you cross the Bridge of Choice you must travel around the Sea of Discipline and Commitment. There is no other way to reach the River of Songs and Real Self. Whatever approach you choose, it will take discipline and commitment to live out of your highest beliefs.

You can use the following process as a basis for your values journal or you can use it as a tool to think through the experiences and conclusions which have lead to your belief systems. Either way you will have the opportunity to contemplate who you are in the light of your beliefs.

As you contemplate your beliefs, consider the topics of truth and wisdom, rights and responsibility, relationships and trust, power and control, life mission and purpose, and finally, what it means to you to live an authentic life.

TRUTH AND WISDOM

What do you believe about truth? The definition of the word can vary from individual to individual. One person may believe that truth is to be manipulated so that she is protected. Another person may believe truth is a synonym for honesty.

Someone else may believe truth is a representation of the life experience. Still another may say that truth is God.

It is important to your understanding of yourself to determine what you believe about truth? To touch your own life experience with truth, take a moment and write down your thoughts. If you have chosen to journal you can use this process to generate thoughts about your values. Now, reach back into your past and think about these questions:

> What are the significant positive experiences from your past when you "told the truth?"

> What are the significant positive experiences from your past when someone discovered you were lying?

> What are the significant negative experiences from your past when you "told the truth?"

> What are the significant negative experiences from your past when someone discovered you were lying?

Years ago when I personally faced myself and answered these questions, I was amazed at my answers. Although everyone in my family and school said they believed people should be truthful, I quickly learned if I told the truth I got negative responses and if I lied well enough people were much happier with me. I knew it was imperative that I never be caught in a lie. So I made sure I never lied when I could be caught. And when I lied I made sure the lie was very close to what actually happened. I ended up getting very positive reinforcement for becoming an excellent liar. To make sure I never got caught in a lie I would just replay the situation in my head the way I said it happened until what I imagined became more real than what actually happened. There is even some question as to whether the human mind knows the difference between what actually happens and what is vividly imagined.

One experience when I remember lying happened around Christmas. I was eleven years old. My brother had just gotten his drivers license. I don't remember the circumstances which placed us in a car stuffed with Christmas presents, but I do remember what happened. He was driving us home. Our house was located twenty miles out of town. There was very little traffic. The backseat was covered with Christmas presents waiting to be opened the next day. In the excitement of the moment we wanted to know which packages were addressed to us. I was leaning over the back seat and reading the tags when my brother, looking at one especially large package addressed to him, drove off the road and into the ditch. Luckily, the ditch was a gradual incline filled with low weeds and brush. The car bounced to an abrupt stop as my brother slammed on the brakes. Terrified we'd wrecked the car, we both jumped out when the car stopped. As we both stood stunned, looking at the car and praying it was unharmed, a stranger seeing two children standing next to a car in the ditch stopped and asked, "What happened?"

In that split second, I knew if I told the truth we'd be in big trouble. Being only eleven and still perfecting my lying ability I could only stammer, "I don't know" which was clearly a lie because I did know. My brother wasn't much better at lying. He sputtered, "The car went out of control. It just went out of control." The stranger showed us how we could easily drive the car out of the ditch and back on the road. By the time we got home we both agreed our parents had no need to know about this experience. So that evening when my Father called us out to the car asking about the scratches he found on the lower side panel, I could say with complete confidence, "I didn't know there were any scratches on the car."

Later in my life I learned it was rare I had to lie about events, but lying about emotions became more natural. Since anger was never an accepted emotion in my first experiences either at home or at school, I learned to lie about my anger. When anyone asked me if I was angry, I would say "no". Then I would explain my concerns or how sad I was about the situation or what I would like to happen, but I would never admit to being angry. It wasn't until a friend said, "Are you aware you smile when you seem angry?" that I realized the extent of my lies. The ultimate lie, is not the lie you tell others, it's the lie you tell yourself. It's the lie you believe. It's when you can't tell your own experience because you lie to yourself.

When I first contemplated these questions about truth, I discovered I couldn't remember a significant positive experience of when I told the truth, but I had many memories of when lying saved me from getting in trouble. I had several significant negative experiences both at home and at school when I told the truth.

One of the first experiences I can remember when I told the truth occurred when I was about 3 years old. My father, a farmer and a veteran of World War II, was offered farm training from the government. If a farmer who was a veteran signed up for the on-the-job training he was given monetary compensation for his time. So my father and many other veteran farmers who had spent their lives farming signed up. When the farm bureau instructor visited our farm he was introduced to me as my father's teacher. I thought my father was the smartest man in the world so I was ready to be impressed by his teacher. I was allowed to watch them work as long as I stayed out of the way. One afternoon as my father and his teacher were working on machinery the teacher threw down a monkey wrench and said in disgust "this wrench doesn't fit." Even at the age of three, I'd been around tools enough to know a monkey wrench has a screw which makes it adjustable. Later, after the teacher had left for the day I heard my father say to my mother, "That idiot doesn't even know how to use a monkey wrench." A few days later when the teacher was leaving, he knelt down beside me and said in a condescending voice "do you have any questions?" I asked politely, "Why don't you know how to use a monkey wrench?" and then I added, "My father thinks you're stupid." Both parents reacted by saying I was mistaken because my father hadn't said anything like that. Later my parents tried to explain what socially acceptable behavior was, but I translated the experience into my understanding about truth. Truth was risky. Truth was something you didn't talk about in public. Truth got me in trouble.

To the best of my recollection I can't remember ever getting caught lying. For the most part I tried to tell the truth until I found out that telling the truth got me into trouble. Then I worked diligently to only tell lies which would never be discovered. All of these experiences brought me to an internal conflict with my own beliefs. When I became an adult, I said I believed that "truth was the best policy," yet from my life experiences I learned that lying had positive outcomes. The question I had to ask myself was: Was I willing to accept the consequences from living out my beliefs about truth?

In my research hundreds of people stated they have a strong belief in speaking the truth. And most admitted they are not able to live according to this belief. Some told me of not being able to speak truthfully to their bosses because of fear of losing their jobs. Others disclosed that although they believed telling the truth was important, they would lie to protect someone's feelings. Almost everyone had experiences at home or school where they had been punished for telling their truth. Some people got into deep discussions about whether there was a difference in lying by deliberately telling a falsehood and lying by omission. Everyone agreed people must have the time to contemplate how their beliefs in truth can be translated into their daily behaviors. Making the commitment and taking the time to contemplate your beliefs about truth, signify you are choosing the path of wisdom. Wisdom is a way of living which uses discernment, knowledge, and insight to bring truth to life.

RIGHTS AND RESPONSIBILITIES

What do you believe about rights and responsibilities?

What are your rights? What defines you?

Where do your rights begin and end?

What are your responsibilities to yourself, to others and the world?

When you understand your past experiences and beliefs about rights and responsibilities, you claim another part of the complex system of your beliefs. Take a moment and write down your thoughts about your experiences with rights and responsibilities.

Rights refer to what you are entitled to or the privileges you have. Your past rights are what you were authorized to do at home and in school. Rights are what you were allowed to do and what you were prohibited from doing.

Responsibilities are the behaviors, roles or duties for which you are answerable. Being responsible means that you are accountable for your conduct and obligations.

If you have chosen to journal you can use these questions and statements to generate your thoughts about your values. If you are not writing out your answers, be sure you allow yourself enough time to think through your answers.

Now, reach back into your past and think about these questions:

What are the significant positive experiences from your past when you were responsible?

What are the significant positive experiences from your past concerning your rights?

What were your rights as a child at home? at school?

What are the significant negative experiences from your past concerning responsibilities?

What are the significant negative experiences from your past concerning your rights?

A right is what we can do. A responsibility is what we are answerable for. The founding fathers of America claimed their beliefs about peoples' rights when they wrote about "inalienable rights" of citizens. During my research many people told me they didn't have "rights" as children or that their "rights" changed according to the mood of their parents. All adults and children should have basic rights: the right to safety and physical boundaries, the right to emotional boundaries, the right to intellectual boundaries, the right to spiritual boundaries, and the right to get our own needs met in a non-harming manner.

Physical boundaries are most often violated by parental violence or neglect. Children, who are touched inappropriately by parents or other adults, frequently must deny their rights to determine how and when people enter their physical space. Many people report that seemingly insignificant rights violation occurred during the holidays when adult relatives hugged them without their permission. Children who experienced situations where adults hugged them in response to their statements: "I don't want to be hugged," learned that some of their "physical rights" were not protected in their families. Years later adults still report feeling angry when they think about how Uncle Henry or Aunt Lucy never even considered that children should have the right to say "no" when someone entered their physical space.

Everyone has the right to experience their own emotions. Notice I did not say everyone has the right to act the way they're feeling. The right to experience what you are feeling is simply: you are allowed to experience your own anger, sadness, joy, etc. and you have the right to determine how you feel about any person or situation. This right allows you not to feel like someone else is feeling. When parents do not clarify that their feelings are their own, children may lose their emotional rights. Many adults tell me their mothers and fathers still say: "I can't be happy if you're not happy." Of course, when their parents were children, they probably learned they had no emotional rights; if Mother was sad, then they must be sad too. Adults who have not determined their emotional rights frequently feel guilty when they are happy. One of my friends frequently protests: "But how can I be happy when there are so many unhappy people around me." She is gradually learning to have compassion for the plight of others without relinquishing her own emotional rights to feel what she is feeling. Emotional rights violations are very common. Daily I hear people say things like: "You shouldn't feel that way, I don't." "You shouldn't be angry." "He didn't mean anything by it." "Please don't cry."

In addition to emotional rights, human beings have the right to intellectual boundaries or the right to think their own thoughts. People have the right to sort through their experiences and determine what they want and need. Of course, young children need help sorting out the facts, but that does not mean an adult should think for them. Even a young child has the right to make some choices. The choice could be whether to wear the white shirt or the red one, but the child's thoughts and choices must be respected, if the child is to learn about her intellectual rights.

One of the negative experiences with my intellectual rights happened one Christmas when I wanted a doll. I don't remember how old I was, but I remember my parents told me I "shouldn't want a doll because I was too old for dolls." This is an example of an intellectual rights violation. I had the right to think about what I wanted and I had the right to want a doll. Notice, I'm not saying I had the right to get a doll for Christmas, but I did have the right to determine what I wanted. To be fair, I later learned that my parents were having financial difficulties and they couldn't afford toys that Christmas. What would have been more appropriate and would not have violated my intellectual boundaries was to have someone explain: "I understand you want a doll for Christmas, but we don't have enough money to buy toys. Most of our Christmas presents will be warm clothing and food. I'm sorry you won't be able to get what you want." These statements would have protected my rights to determine what I wanted.

When I didn't get a doll for Christmas, I blamed myself for wanting the wrong things. Then, with other experiences like these over the years, I learned not to want anything. It took me years as an adult to even figure out what I like to do because as a child I had lost my rights to determine my own needs and wants.

Spiritual rights are difficult to explain and crucial to the development of a child's self esteem. Human beings have the right to believe in a higher Power Who loves them. When someone tells a child, God will not love her unless she acts a certain way, the child's right to believe in a higher Power Who loves her unconditionally, is violated. Adults have the right to determine their own beliefs about their spirituality. Every child has the right to believe in a God Who loves her just as she is. Spiritual rights are violated when a child feels that her mistakes make her unworthy of God's love or that she must be perfect to avoid being judged by God as a mistake. Children need to grow up with the concept of a God Who loves them unconditionally.

All children make mistakes. Children need to know their parents and God will love them and forgive them when they make mistakes. When religions or people tell children, they "will go to hell for what they think or how they feel," the children often live in a state of terror believing they are defective.

Spiritual rights are also violated when parents or teachers threaten children with God's punishment. When a child's view of a God Who loves her unconditionally is destroyed, she develops a view of God as violent, unpredictable and punishing. It should be no surprise to anyone that children who grow up believing in a judgmental, punishing God often turn into judgmental, punishing parents. If spiritual rights are violated as a child, the adult will have difficulty being able to embrace and love herself.

An associate of mine, who was raised in a very strict religious family, believed God would punish children for thinking "bad thoughts." When she was about four years old she believed she was magical. This magical thinking stage is natural for young children. Somehow her magical thinking and her belief about God punishing her for thinking bad thoughts collided. She believed all she had to do was think about something and it would happen and God would punish her. She tried very hard but she couldn't stop thinking about things she wanted to happen. Somehow at this very young age she figured out that God would judge her as evil because she believed in magical thinking. This belief became part of her Original Map. She still judges herself from that Original Map. And although she is beginning to like herself, she admits she is still unable to truly love herself since the Original Map haunts her with the message that God judged her, at the age of four, as evil.

During my interviews with people about their spiritual rights an individual told me that the song, *Jesus Loves Me*, was a positive significant experience in his spiritual rights development. The idea of a song designed just to let children know they are loved by a Power greater than themselves still brings a smile to his face.

We also have the right to get our needs met. Everyone has the right to pursue non-harming actions to get their needs met. We cannot harm others in the pursuit of our needs, but we do have the right to live our lives in such a way as to get our needs for food, clothing, shelter, love, belonging and self actualization met. As children, many of us realized our needs were unimportant and often embarrassing. A woman, nearing fifty years of age, told me about a negative experience in second grade concerning a basic rights violation. She remembers it was her birthday and her parents had given her new cowboy boots. She wore them to school. During the morning session she raised her hand and asked to be excused to go to the bathroom. But the teacher was fed up with all the requests for bathroom privileges that morning so she said "no." The woman remembers she was forced to stand in front of the class. She can't forget the feeling of urine running down her legs into her new cowboy boots. Tears still form in her eyes when she tells the story about this early basic rights violation.

As you contemplate your values, be sure to ask yourself questions about your experiences concerning physical, emotional, intellectual and spiritual rights. Try writing your own descriptions for each of the rights, or answer the questions:

What do physical rights mean to you?

What are your beliefs about your emotional and spiritual rights?

What intellectual rights do you have in your life at present?

Determine past significant negative and positive experiences concerning your physical rights, your emotional rights, your intellectual rights and your spiritual rights.

My research reveals that people remember many more negative experiences than positive ones. In fact many people are at a loss to come up with any positive experiences about their rights. Frequently the reason our rights were violated by our parents or teachers is that their rights were violated by their parents or teachers when they were children. It seems that many of us as children had our basic rights so violated, that we have trouble understanding our rights today as adults.

It is impossible to talk about rights without talking about responsibilities. Your responsibilities are the obligations you assume in your life and the commitments you make to yourself and others. To understand your beliefs about responsibilities, contemplate the questions:

What are your responsibilities to yourself?

What are your commitments to yourself?

What are your responsibilities to others? What are your obligations to others?

What are your responsibilities to the organization where you work?

What are your obligations to your co-workers?

What are your responsibilities to the world you live in?

One of the best ways to unpack the answers to these questions, is to focus on the significant positive and negative experiences from your past concerning responsibilities.

As a child, I can think of several positive experiences I had concerning responsibilities. At home and at school I was rewarded for living responsibly. At school we even had charts to track how well we lived up to our work contracts. We contracted to turn in our homework by 10:00 the morning after it was assigned. I earned an award for having the best track record for turning in homework.

A gentleman around forty years of age told me his most memorable experience concerning responsibilities. He was an active nine year old who tried hard to follow his parents' numerous rules, but, like most nine year olds, he made mistakes. When he made mistakes, his parents would chastise him by telling him he should grow up and be more responsible. Wanting to gain his parents love and approval he decided that he would prove to them how responsible he was.

For weeks he kept watching for the right situation to prove to his parents he really was a responsible person. One day, as his parents drove past a peach orchard they had on their property, he heard his father remark to his mother, it would soon be time to pick the peaches. Both his mother and father bemoaned the fact they didn't have the time or energy to pick peaches in the hot sun. When he heard this, the nine year old knew he had his opportunity. He wanted to surprise them so he set to work in secret. He spent an entire day from 6:00 in the morning until after dusk picking peaches. At the end of the day he was physically exhausted, but emotionally proud of his accomplishment. After lugging bushels of peaches up to the steps, he called his parents out to see his handiwork, ready to prove how responsible he was. His parents exploded in anger and frustration when they saw the still green peaches placed so carefully in the baskets.

At forty he still admits he is cautious about taking on any responsibilities without considering every aspect of a situation. His first experiences about responsibilities taught him that he could get in serious trouble if he tried to be responsible. He says he believes in responsible living and he finds himself feeling angry when people around him don't behave in a responsible manner.

Many people tell me of negative experiences concerning responsibilities in their families and at school. One women who was the oldest child in a large family told me: "I never had a childhood. I was responsible for changing diapers before I could dress a doll. Whenever I sat down my father would tell me to go help my mother. All I remember about being a child is being continually tired because I was responsible for so many children. When I was around thirteen years old my parents took a two week vacation and left me in charge of my five brothers and one sister. At the time my sister wasn't even a year old. The only year we had a family vacation my brother got sick. My parents went on the vacation with my brothers and sister and I stayed home taking care of my sick brother. Since both my parents worked, I was responsible for cooking, cleaning and running the house. But when I got a job in high school it didn't end. I went to school, worked at a restaurant after school, and when I came home I still did the cooking, cleaning, and washing for my brothers. Today, I still feel responsible for everyone. I know rationally that I'm not responsible for other people, but I still feel responsible. When I see people who do not act in a responsible manner toward their children, I feel incredible anger."

One man told me his school responsibilities ended up being a significant negative experience. He went to a school that had a large ratio of students to teachers. Because he was naturally good at reading and math, he became a teacher's helper. For most of his grade school years he helped other children, frequently at the expense of his own studies. He got a lot of positive reinforcement for his helping behaviors. Today as an adult he recognizes he often neglects his own needs to the detriment of his health and well being to meet the needs of others. It's not that he doesn't value helping others, but he is trying to balance his own needs with the needs of others. He finds this difficult because he learned in his first experiences with responsibility that others' needs were more important than his and he would be rewarded only when he placed the needs of his classmates before his own.

As way of understanding your beliefs and experiences about your rights and responsibilities, experiment with writing your own personal "bill of rights and responsibilities." Several years ago, as I focused on understanding my values, I realized that I didn't have a clear understanding of my own physical, emotional, intellectual and spiritual rights. So I wrote my personal "bill of rights and responsibilities." I will share part of it with you, not because I think it will work for you, but because I believe you can use it as a sample to develop your own bill of rights and responsibilities. Each person can determine her own past experiences and present beliefs by asking the question: "What are my experiences and beliefs concerning my rights and responsibilities?" As you experiment with developing your own statements, remember your rights entitle you to the basic dignity which is the privilege of all human beings and your responsibilities make you answerable for 100% of your behavior.

SAMPLE: Bill of Rights and Responsibilities

Rights

I have the right to determine who touches me. I have the right to feel my own emotions. I have the right to think my own thoughts. I have the right to believe in a higher Power Who loves me unconditionally. I have the right to meet my own needs for food, clothing, shelter, love, belonging and self actualization as long as I am not harming myself or others.

Rights Concerning Others

Other people have the right to determine who touches them. I will ask permission either verbally or nonverbally before I touch someone. Other people have the right to feel their own emotions. I will not expect others to share the same emotions I have. I will honor the emotions they feel by not asking them to feel differently for me. Others have the right to think their own thoughts. I will not tell others what I think they should think. I do not have to agree with their thinking but I will respect their right to think their own thoughts. Other people have the right to determine their own spiritual beliefs. I do not have to agree with their beliefs, but I will respect their right to determine the higher Power they choose to worship. I recognize that other people have the right to pursue getting their needs met for food, clothing, shelter, love, belonging and self actualization.

Responsibilities: Dealing with Rights Violations

I will not allow anyone to violate my rights or to abuse me. If I perceive this is occurring I have the following responsibilities to take care of myself: I can ask them to stop or I can excuse myself and leave. I am not responsible for managing their behavior. I am only responsible for maintaining my rights in the most non-harming way to myself and to others involved.

Responsibilities: Dealing with Others

I am not responsible for the behavior of any adult human being except myself. I will not rescue people from the natural consequences of their irresponsible behaviors. I will not finance others' irresponsible behaviors. I will not lie to protect myself or others from the consequences of their behaviors. I believe people are responsible for their own behaviors, therefore, I will not try to fix others and I will not allow others to try to fix me. I will take 100% responsibility for my behaviors and for my own personal growth and development. I accept responsibility for determining how my time, money, energy, and attention will be spent. I accept responsibility for the periodic review of my rights and responsibilities so they represent my beliefs.

RELATIONSHIPS AND TRUST

What beliefs do you have about relationships?

Human relationships can be four fold: people can have a relationship with themselves, with others, with nature and with God.

What constitutes a relationship in your life?

How do you determine whether or not you trust yourself, someone else, nature or God?

What is your basic perspective toward relationships? Are you open to growing and learning or are you protective of yourself?

Everyone has a general perspective toward their four types of relationships: they are either open or closed. An open outlook motivates people toward learning while a closed perspective motivates them toward protecting themselves. Figure 3 shows the result of each perspective.

Learning behaviors result in openness to "telling your own story" and "hearing the story of the other party." These behaviors are characterized by openness to personal growth, curiosity, gentle humor, personal accountability and responsibility, truthfulness about your own experiences and feelings, and a compassion toward others with a respectful distance. The distance reminds you that "their experiences belong to them." It is not respectful to go wading around in other people's experiences trying to make them your own.

The first time I remember noticing this openness was with my nephew. He was in second grade. His brother was in kindergarten. Their mother and I were helping them make valentines for their classmates. The older brother was painstakingly cutting out each heart. The younger brother was madly slapping pieces of red on white paper doilies. Each time the youngest finished another valentine, he showed it to his mother, who promptly gave him positive recognition. Suddenly the older brother exploded with anger. Startled, his mother told him to go to his room and cool down. After a few moments, I asked if she'd mind if I talked to him. With her permission, I went to his bedroom door, knocked and asked very gently if I could come in. I could barely hear the voice that whispered "yes." I'll never forget his large blue eyes and how he closely watched every move I made. His forehead was furrowed and his lips were pressed tightly together. "Do you mind if I just sit with you for a minute?" I asked. He shook his head no. I asked him to tell his story, "Will you tell me what happened?" When he didn't say anything, I told him part of my story, "I sometimes feel icky when other people do things faster than I do them. I know it's because I like to do things so that they look just right. But it's still a pretty

GENERAL PERSPECTIVES

CLOSED	OPEN
MOTIVATED TOWARD PROTECTION BEHAVIORS	**MOTIVATED TOWARD LEARNING BEHAVIORS**
Judging	Openness to Personal Growth
Blaming	Curiosity
Put Downs	Gentle Humor
Sarcasm	Personal Accountability and Responsibility
Fixing Others	
Controlling	Truthfulness about Self
Power Plays	Compassion with Distance
CONSEQUENCES	**CONSEQUENCES**
Loss of Trust for Self and Others	Authenticity
Speaking Falsehoods	Learning
Anger, Pain	Satisfaction
Frustration	Freedom to be Yourself

Figure 3

uncomfortable feeling when someone competes with me and I am slower." His eyes sparkled with tears as he nodded his head and whispered, "I feel that way too." We talked for a while longer, then I told him my story about what I do to make myself feel better. I asked him what he thought would work for him. He used some of my ideas and added some of his own. By the time we left the room we'd worked out a strategy to help him deal with the situation. Most importantly, we had both learned.

Imagine that same situation with me operating from a closed perspective using protection behaviors. I could have walked into his room and said, "You're a bad boy. You shouldn't get angry at your brother. You should love your brother. You'd better fix that attitude, young man, because I'm not going to put up with any more of this behavior." You probably recognize the protection behaviors of judging, blaming, put downs and controlling.

A more subtle protection behavior is "fixing others." If I'd used fixing behaviors, the same situation might have sounded like this: "You poor thing. I know it's hard to be around your brother. You just need to tune him out. If you just learn to ignore him you'll feel a whole lot better." Fixing behaviors often look like sympathy and concern, but they always end up telling you to be different. If you were "fixed" you wouldn't have the problem.

Fixing behaviors operate on the assumption that someone else knows more about how you should live than you do. Someone else is in the superior position and you are the one who needs help. The superior person doesn't need to change because they have the answers to your life. The person in the superior position doesn't need to learn or grow, all she has to do is come up with answers for your life. The superior person operates from a protected space because she doesn't need to face herself. In the superior role it's always easier to focus on someone else's problems than honestly face your own.

The consequences from living in a closed, protective perspective are always the same. Living a life focused on protecting yourself leads to pain. The consequences from living in an open, learning perspective are often painful in the beginning but sooner or later lead to authenticity.

It is important to determine what experiences influenced your past beliefs and behaviors and what you believe today about relationships and trust. Reach back into your past and think about these questions:

What are the significant positive relationship experiences from your past?

What significant positive experiences from your past occurred when you trusted someone?

What are the significant negative relationship experiences from your past?

What significant negative experiences from your past occurred when you trusted someone?

The first relationships you formed as a child may give you the basis for your relationships for the rest of your life. The first relationships become part of the Original Map. Some people report that their first relationships still haunt their adult lives. For example, children of divorced families often have more concerns about lasting relationships than other children. Thankfully, many people report they had at least one person they bonded with when they were children. It is critically important for a child to bond with at least one person as this bond will be her first experience of trust. Children who do not bond with anyone may not be able to have trusting relationships later in their lives. Children who bond with a parent who abuses them may learn that relationships include abuse. When the abused child becomes an adult, she may have a range of behaviors she will use to protect herself from any relationship, or she may enter into relationships which repeat the abusive pattern. Either way the Original Map must be retranslated for her to begin having healthy adult relationships.

Any situation which repeats itself in your life can be used as a metaphor for gaining information about yourself. For example, Cynthia has had seven car accidents in the last ten years. She has also broken a toe twice and consistently burns herself when she cooks. She has had a complete physical and agrees nothing is wrong with her physically. She does, however, admit that all these experiences form a pattern in her life; she doesn't pay attention when her safety is involved. None of the accidents occurred when anyone else was in the car. Her similar experiences can be viewed as a metaphor in the shape of a question: What past experiences does she have that lead her to believe she does not have the right or responsibility for making sure she is physically safe? It may take Cynthia weeks, months, or even years to answer the question and retranslate her experience to "I deserve to be physically safe and I am capable of keeping myself safe."

Although any life experience can be a metaphor, relationships are frequently the most powerful metaphor for many people. Consider the metaphor of how you treat yourself.

Do you take care of your physical needs in a healthy manner?

Do you pay attention to your feelings?

Do you comfort yourself when you are sad; celebrate yourself when you are joyful?

The metaphor of how you treat yourself will give you a wealth of information about the type of relationship you have with yourself. Many people tell me the relationship with self is the relationship most often neglected.

Your relationships with others probably involve a set of complex beliefs. You may believe your sense of well-being comes first. You may believe that being nice is the basis for all relationships. You may believe your relationships with your group (family, organization, church, etc.) come first. Or, you may believe you must honor and respect the needs of all others and yourself. What you believe about your relationships with others will determine the type of perspective you bring to the relationship, the roles you will play, the way you will meet your needs for love and belonging and how you will interact in social environments.

Many people do not realize they have a relationship with nature, which may be one of the reasons so many scientists are warning us about the need to change human behaviors. Humans seem to have an incredible ability to harm the air they breathe, the water they drink, and other natural resources they need to live. The relationship with nature addresses the connection you have with the natural world around you.

Do you believe the natural world of air, water, trees, plants and animals is there only to serve you?

Do you believe your rights to the natural environment should be protected?

Do you believe the natural environment should be saved for your children?

Do you believe you have responsibilities for the natural environment?

How do you play out your relationship with nature? Do you own a boat? Do you plant flowers? Do you recycle your garbage?

Do you use natural resources sparingly? Have you considered your beliefs and your connection to nature as part of the complex equation of "who you are?"

Finally, what is your relationship to your higher power? Do you trust the universe?

A famous man once said the most important question in life is "Is the universe friendly?" Do you believe the universe is friendly? You have the right as an adult to develop the personal relationship you want with your higher Power. Determining what you believe about your spirituality will offer you the basis for your relationship with your higher Power.

POWER AND CONTROL

Most children learned they were powerless or had very limited power when it came to the authorities in their lives. I still see the impact of these experiences when people tell me they are afraid of authority figures. They are afraid to give "bad news" to their bosses. They are afraid of asking their spouses if they can go to a workshop. They are uncomfortable when their supervisor corrects a mistake.

At a recent board meeting, two board members were talking when the chairman of the board barked "Will you two pipe down!" Everyone at the meeting lowered their eyes in reaction to this obvious display of power and control. Power is the ability to control yourself, people and the environment. What are your beliefs and experiences about power? Some people believe power goes with a role such as president, parent, teacher, etc. Other people like to be in power both at work and at home. Still others believe power is the ability to govern yourself.

It is important to determine what you believe about power and control. Remember, if you have chosen to journal, you can ask these questions to generate thoughts about your values concerning power and control.

Now, reach back into your past and think about these questions:

What are the significant positive experiences from your past concerning authority?

What are the significant positive experiences from your past when you felt empowered?

What are the significant negative experiences from

your past when you felt someone or something else was in control?

What are the significant negative experiences from your past when you tried to control people or situations?

Many twelve step programs address the problems which stem from controlling behaviors. I personally have been amazed to discover that the more I let go of trying to control events or people outside myself, the more positive my experiences are. What I learned is, trying to control the future brings me pain. The best way I can describe my experience with control is to tell you the parable I wrote for myself.

The River Parable

When I was born into the great river of life, my parents were concerned I would drown, so like many other parents, they placed me in a canoe and taught me to paddle up stream. The one skill I developed as a child was that I could "paddle like hell." I was so busy paddling I didn't notice I wasn't going anywhere; for the nature of the river of life is that it always flows as fast as you paddle.

One day I grew so weary with paddling, I got sick. As I lay in my canoe dying, the current lightly touched the canoe and turned it so I faced down stream. As I recovered, I was astonished at how easy it was to ride the current down stream. But after a while I noticed a large boulder looming ahead . Since I'd spent my whole life heading up stream and getting no where, I'd never seen a boulder before. I relied on my one best skill. As soon as I saw the boulder I started paddling like hell. Now I was headed down stream but whenever I saw anything that looked like a boulder, a snag or choppy water, I paddled like hell. After a while I felt as tired heading downstream as I had when I'd been heading upstream. The difference was that I was moving.

Then one day, when I was in an area of the stream with no visible trouble, I considered my paddling behavior and wondered if there might be a better way to live. After some contemplation, I figured out I could sit quietly in the canoe and watch the currents. I became mindful of the way the currents broke around the troublesome spots. I began to be able to read the river. I began to get a sense of my own skills and how the canoe moved. I stopped trying to overpower the river. Finally, after much practice, I learned to sit quietly in my canoe when a boulder appears, to wait until I am almost on top of the boulder, then, at the last minute, to slip my paddle into the water and let the canoe effortlessly glide by.

MISSION AND PURPOSE

What is your life work?

What are your beliefs about your work?

What do you want to do "on purpose" in your life?

Abraham Maslow studied and described people who were fully engaged in their work and their lives, people who continued to grow in self awareness, self trust, and self esteem. Maslow called these people self actualizing. Self actualizing simply means growing toward wholeness. These people continuously risk by being truthful, following their wisdom, claiming their rights, owning their responsibilities and empowering themselves and others. They are committed to making sure their outer lives are integrated with their inner beliefs. For people who are self actualizing, their work is an expression of Real Self and love. The work they choose to do enriches them. Joseph Campbell speaks of this as "bliss" in the book *The Power of Myth*. He says, "I always tell my students, go where your body and soul wants to go. When you have the feeling, then stay with it, and don't let anyone throw you off. We are having experiences all the time .... a little intuition of where your bliss is. Grab it. No one can tell you what it is going to be. You have to learn to recognize your own depth."

You not only "have to learn to recognize your own depth" to follow your bliss, you also have to accept that your attitudes, abilities and talents are your blueprint for leading a life of bliss. Choosing to follow your bliss means you stop looking to others to tell you your purpose and you enter into whatever work you can do with mindfulness. Mindfulness is the quality of being fully present in your own life.

Many of us had our life work chosen for us by parents, teachers and advisors. They made the very best choices they could, but more than likely the profession you are engaged in right now is not "following your bliss." The ability to choose the work you do is one of the most significant choices you will make in your life. It is painful for adults to admit, they did not choose their professions and they are not following their bliss. It takes incredible courage for adults to correct the past and make new conscious choices about work. An adult must consciously choose the work she will do if she is to follow her bliss. This doesn't mean you have to quit your job, although you may choose to do so. It's really up to you. You get to determine the work which follows your bliss and how to bring it into your life.

Discovering your own mission and purpose may be the hardest task of all. Experts, media, financial planners, career counselors, teachers, parents and friends, just to name a few, tell us what we should do to be happy. Yet, there is no way for anyone else to know what your true "purpose" is. Living "on purpose" is using your work as a natural way to express who you are. It is dishonoring of yourself to disregard "who you are" when you go to work each day.

People who risk taking their hearts to work with them declare something remarkable happens to them. They are afraid at first; then their self expression breeds greater confidence.   The outcome is that customers respond more positively, conflicts are brought out into the open and solved and employees become more trusting.   Some people tell me they think others are just waiting for someone to be authentic because it gives them permission to be more real, too.

6

The Dragons

"Perhaps all the dragons of our lives are princesses who are only waiting to see us once beautiful and brave."

Rainer Marie Rilke

If you want to be confident, make peace with your dragons.

Everyone has dragons. They feed on the emotions and actions which rise from our fears. In the beginning when we were children our fears protected us. As children who depended on others for survival our fears were often necessary and helpful to us. The natural fear response protects children when situations feel unsafe to them. During childhood, most fear responses became part of the Original Map. By adulthood, the dragons live in the forest of daily life patterns waiting for the time when they can roar.

In the fairy tales I read as a child I remember dragons always had to be dealt with before the "happily ever after" occurred. The dragon was the symbol of the fear, or roadblock, which prevented the hero from living out his life in peace and harmony.

Dragons are the natural fears which can negatively motivate people to engage in a range of destructive behaviors. You'll know whenever you approach your dragons by the anxiety you experience.

Since I've heard my own dragons roar in outrage, I now recognize when others have released theirs. I saw a dragon freed one afternoon when I was talking with a colleague. As we ate lunch, she talked about a painful experience. A committee she was leading had threatened a revolt. She explained what was happening: "Three committee members are threatening to quit and form their own group. Everyone thinks I'm over controlling the meetings, but I think they're being irresponsible. Last week I got a phone call from the printer. No one had called to tell him the color for the brochure. So, I made the decision. Now everyone is angry with me because I made the decision without asking them but, at least I'm getting things done."

She admitted that their rejection of her as their leader bothered her. She said she'd like to learn better ways to work with her committee and she confessed she'd like to improve her meetings. Then, as her dragon awoke, she asked me what I did at my meetings?

Long ago I learned people must help themselves. I do not have the answers to someone's life problems. Each human, if he is honest with himself, knows himself better than anyone else. If he listens to himself, he will find his best solutions.

One of the very best way adults learn is when they share their experiences. Usually, I listen from my heart to what is said and not said. Then I share my own experiences. In the quiet space which follows the telling of our stories, we can each determine what we've learned. Each person's right to decide his own solutions is protected.

I answered her question by first explaining that I didn't know what would work for her. Then I offered to share my own experiences with the condition that she had the responsibility for deciding if there was anything worthwhile for her in my story.

I explained, "I start preparing for my meetings about two weeks before they occur when I send out a letter asking for everyone's agenda items. From their responses I set up an initial agenda. At the meeting I hand out the agenda and ask if anyone has anything to add. Then I ask my committee members to prioritize the list. Then we start the meeting with their top priority and ..." In the middle of my sentence her dragon roared.

She exploded, "I don't have time to waste. If I do all that I'll never get anything else done. Besides I want to write the agenda. It's the only way I can keep everyone in line. I know what should happen at my meetings. I'm the one who's in charge. If you think I'm going to ask them what they want on the agenda, think again. They're trying to take over now. And, you're suggesting I help them. They'd walk all over me. Maybe you don't care if people walk over you, but no one walks over me."

During her tirade, my dragon lifted her head and sniffed the air but I tickled her chin and said to her, "Go back to sleep. This is not serious. I respect and honor your energy and will not waste it just because her dragon is loose." When she finished her harangue I said gently, "It sounds like you didn't find anything useful in my experience." Later she telephoned and made amends, "I was out of line, but I can't believe how calm you stayed. I was almost yelling at you."

While making peace with my dragons, I learned quite a bit about them. Dragons in general are very fierce and can overpower you quite easily. Dragons love to eat. They feed on the human emotions which result from fear.

Emotions are very valuable. They let us know when something is wrong. When we feel angry, the anger is a signal that we need to pay attention to what is happening to us. When we are sad, the sadness is an indication of our experience. Each emotion is an important indication of what we feel in the moment.

Some people are so fearful of feeding their dragons they shut off their emotions. They stop feeling. But no one can stop feeling for long. The emotions build until the dragon rages out of control and then, they can't stop him from feeding.

When I first met my dragons they were used to feeding on my emotions. The moment I felt anger the dragon was eating. Then in a split second I'd be riding the dragon, flying off in all directions. The hot dragon flames burned several of my friends and relatives and I had to work to regain their trust.

To make peace with my dragons I had to get to know them. First, I had to discover and acknowledge my fears which created them. Then I had to develop a method of hearing my emotions without feeding my dragons. Finally, I had to honor them for the good work they do.

Most people make the mistake of thinking that all their fears come from events outside themselves. If you are clinging to the side of a cliff and feeling fearful about falling, you are right when you suppose the fear is generated from the situation. But, in many cases, the fears living inside each of us are merely triggered by outside events. The fears themselves come from within; these are the dragons who reside in the forest of our daily life patterns.

I remember a telephone conversation with a co-worker. He asked me if I had worked with a mutual colleague. When I answered, "Yes," he asked me what I thought of her. I said I could only offer my experiences. I told him about the three projects we'd worked on together and finished by saying, "I enjoyed working with her and learned quite a bit about myself from the experience. What I admired most about her was they way she handled a conflict. She was careful to listen to all the parties involved and she acknowledged the role she played in the situation. Together we resolved the conflict and remained on good terms with everyone involved."

Then his dragon roared. He asserted, "You're wrong. She's horrible. I worked with her five years ago and I still feel hurt by her. She said she'd help me, instead, she talked about me behind my back. She even got me kicked off a project. She's a vile person." When he finished his diatribe I quietly asked him why he was interested in my experience, since he'd already had his own episode. But his dragon was too fired up and he could no longer hear me. He spent some minutes trying to convince me that my experience was wrong and the person in contention was vile.

It was obvious to me that his dragon was triggered just by thinking about the individual in question. In the beginning his anger may have been in response to events. But the events were five years old; his anger and fear were now internally generated. His dragon was well fed. I learned a lot about myself from the conversation. I learned when others try to convince me that my experiences are wrong my dragon is almost unmanageable. I wanted to roar back, "How dare you tell me I should accept your experience with this person and deny my own. How dare you try to tell me my own experiences of my life are wrong." To say this, would have been to ride my dragon and feed him from my anger. Instead I remained quiet and watched the anger in me until it began to fade, then I calmly spoke: "I respect your negative experience with this individual. I am sorry you are still feeling hurt and angry about her. I am not willing to talk with you if you continue to raise your voice and deny my experiences." He grew more angry and abusive. I said "goodbye" and ended the conversation. I realize I had many options to choose from in this situation. This one was most appropriate for me. The outcome from this conversation is my co-worker doesn't call as often and there is more distance in our relationship. To be truthful, I am satisfied with this outcome. I choose not to have close relationships with people who allow their angry dragons to roam freely.

I am always amazed at the passionate pleas people present when they are trying to convince you to annul your own life experience and accept theirs. Perhaps they do not realize that to deny someone his experience or to ask him to renounce the events of his own life is disrespectful of his spirit. For many people their own dragon wakes when others try to rewrite their lives. To deal effectively with other people's dragons, first make peace with your own.

FEARS THAT CREATE DRAGONS

Everyone has fears. Fear is a response which has been helpful to human survival for hundreds and hundreds of years. Each individual has his own unique fears. These may vary according to their Original Map, their needs and their beliefs. Think back through several situations when you felt anxious. Look for the patterns of your fear in each situation. Name the fear or fears that feed your dragons. Read through the following list of common fears. The words may not fit you exactly, so find the fears that fit you best and then rewrite them so they fit you precisely. When you write down an exact description of your fears, you name your dragon. A dragon with a name is much easier to manage.

COMMON FEARS

I feel most distressed when I am not in charge.

I feel most distressed when other people appear to be arranging things to benefit them and not me.

I feel most distressed when my power to sway other people doesn't seem to work.

I feel most distressed when I don't perform the way I intend to.

I feel most distressed when my work doesn't live up to my expectations.

I feel most distressed when others don't include me.

I feel most distressed when others reject my friendly overtures.

I feel most distressed when people don't like me.

I feel most distressed when I lose friendships.

I feel most distressed when I am bored with the situation or people.

I feel most distressed when I am forced to stay in one spot.

I feel most distressed when other people are angry or under tension.

I feel most distressed when I lose or look bad.

I feel most distressed when things or people are unpredictable.

I feel most distressed when there is disorganization or confusion.

I feel most distressed when there is discord or conflict.

I feel most distressed when I'm not personally advancing and improving.

I feel most distressed when people criticize what I'm doing.

I feel most distressed when people are too friendly.

I feel most distressed when people expect me to get emotionally involved.

I feel most distressed when I lose control of my emotions.

I feel most distressed when something affects my good feelings about what I do.

I feel most distressed when I am conflicted about pleasing myself or pleasing others.

I feel most distressed when people in my group don't respect or admire me.

I feel most distressed when I don't live up to what I say I believe.

In addition to these fears many of us bring with us the common fears from childhood: the fear of letting go, the fear of making mistakes, the fear of being wrong, the fear of failure and the fear of not being worthy.

The emotions which arrive with the fear are frequently overpowering. It often seems as if it is impossible to live through the painful emotions of grief, anger and shame. The truth is we can live through our emotions.

Emotions are feelings. The problem occurs when we start to allow our emotions to overpower us. When the emotion is out of control, we loose touch with our center of being. We are literally "off center." To stay centered you must remember "who you are."

Emotions are only temporary. Emotions change; they rise and fall according to the situation. Emotions are brief and momentary unless you choose to feed them to your dragon. Emotions are signals which help us determine what is happening to us. We can recognize and honor our emotions without feeding the dragons.

Most people haven't ever observed their emotions. The first time you try it, it can be enlightening. Find a quiet place. Quiet your body, and your mind. Go to your internal quiet spot and replay a situation from your past which generated an emotion of anger or sadness. Do not choose an intense, "I'll-never-forget-it-because-it-was-so-awful" situation.

In your mind's eye, play the situation with you as an actor. Then play it with you as an observer watching yourself and the others involved. Then stop and listen to yourself. Pay attention to the different emotions you generated. If emotions arise, choose not to feed them to your dragon. Instead remain an observer and watch them. The emotions will act much like a stream running through your consciousness. See the emotion, watch it rise and fall in intensity as you remain an observer. Be sure to observe how your body acts. Watch for any signs of tension. You may find your throat getting tight or your shoulders starting to bunch. Recognize the reaction and observe it. Remember and honor this reaction as a signal you give to yourself. This signal is you communicating with yourself about what has happened. Store this signal so that you recognize it when it occurs in real time. Allow the emotion, like a stream, to flow out of you. Let yourself go back to your peaceful spot and reflect on what you have learned about your emotions.

This process of watching your emotions is fairly easy to do when you are in a quiet space and reviewing past situations. If you practice with situations from the past, you will begin to develop the habit of observing your emotions. Then, in daily safe situations, start watching your emotions. You may find they rise and fall quite a bit during the day. For example, when you find out your insurance covers your garage fire, you will notice your emotion of relief or gladness rise. Then, the phone may ring and someone may start complaining and your emotion may change to irritation or even anger. By spending time observing your emotions you will learn much about how emotions ebb and flow through you. It usually takes months, sometimes years of doing this to actually watch emotions during intense conflict and not feed them to your dragons.

One word of caution, there are times you will want to feed your dragon. If your life is in danger and you choose to fight, your anger will feed your dragon and your dragon will help protect you. I see nothing wrong with feeding your dragons as long as you consciously make the choice and accept 100% responsibility for your behaviors.

Making peace with your dragons means that you:

1. Recognize that your emotions are not you, they are important signals which you can choose to act upon or not.

2. Develop the discipline to observe your emotions and honor the information they give you.

3. Consciously choose your actions in response to your emotions. You can choose to confront, leave, allow the emotions to flow through, look at the situation from the other person's point of view or feed your dragon.

4. Are 100% responsible for your actions.

7

Wisdom

"Knowledge appears when you understand theories and concepts. Insight appears when you speak your own experience. True wisdom begins to appear when you integrate knowledge and insight."

Real Self is not some idealized state of enlightenment that only a few achieve. Ordinary people travel the inner road to Real Self. Ordinary people answer the question "Who am I?" These are people engaged in deep relationships with themselves. They are courageous people who walk the Road of Awareness and live by the River of Songs.

Many people in their desire to express Real Self ask the question: "How do I get there?" This question focuses people's attention outside themselves so that much time and effort is spent trying to figure out how they should change, where they should go, what goal they should set, how they should interact, etc. The question, How do I get there? assumes there is somewhere to "get."

People who have worked with athletes in peak performance training tell me athletes rarely ask "How do I get to be an Olympic winner?" instead they ask the critical question, "What prevents me from being the best?" For those of us committed to the inner life journey, the most important question we can ask is: "What prevents me from being my Real Self?" The answer to this question will guide each of us to next step in our journey.

The first time I asked myself this question my answer was "perfection." My need to be perfect, to have perfect results prevented me from being my Real Self. To surrender my need to be perfect, I first had to grieve the loss of an ideal. I had to admit I would never be perfect; I would always make mistakes. But most importantly for me, I had to forgive myself for not being perfect. To this day, I still start every day by forgiving myself for not being perfect, thus freeing myself to be Real.

Many people in my life have told me about their personal battles with perfection. Each battle has a different slant. One of my friends is so concerned about painting the perfect picture she can't enjoy the process of painting. When she asked me what I do about perfectionism in my writing, I explained that each day before I start I forgive myself for not writing the perfect letter, article or book. If I didn't forgive myself for not creating the perfect book, I'd never be able to write.

A colleague of mine tells me in his battle with perfection he has to know all the answers or he feels unworthy. He must know every answer to any question so he can prove he's perfect.

Another friend discloses that her battle for perfection involves people. Having her friends think she is socially perfect is what prevents her from being authentic around people. So she tells people what they want to hear and she does what others think she should do. The perfection plays itself out like this: everyone must think she is socially able to positively handle any situation. This means any conflict or discussion she is unable to resolve happily for everyone involved is a painful indicator that she is lacking.

Other people tell me that perfection is not what prevents them from being real. They tell me one of the most common roadblocks is "getting stuck" in past childhood experiences. For example, I met an individual seven years ago. At the time he told me he was dealing with his past childhood issues: anger at his father who was mentally ill and unresolved issues with his mother who didn't protect him from his father's violent rages. It was a heartbreaking story of abuse and neglect. When he told it, I could see his rage and pain. Last year I saw him again for the first time since I'd met him. He told me he'd just divorced his fourth wife. He said it all stemmed from his horrible childhood and his anger at his father who was mentally ill and unresolved issues with his mother who didn't protect him from his father's violent rages. I imagine when I meet him in another seven years I'll hear the same story unless he manages to get unstuck. I don't want to discount his experiences in his childhood. I am positive they were horrible. But no one has a perfect childhood. There is no such thing as a perfect parent. Parents don't have perfect childhoods either. Sheldon Kopp in his partial list of eternal truths states it this way: "Childhood is a nightmare."

To a greater or lesser extent everyone's childhood was a nightmare. It takes incredible open hearted courage to face the nightmare, grieve and comfort yourself, and go on with your life. If you are facing the pain of your childhood experiences, be gentle with yourself, be courageous at facing the past and recounting it honestly to yourself, and give yourself all the time you need. However, be honest with yourself if the years start to pile up and you are still grieving the same situations over and over. Truthfully ask yourself "What prevents me from being my Real Self?" If you answer, "I'm stuck in my past unresolved childhood experiences" then start asking yourself some pointed questions: "What do I get out of being stuck?" "Do I get attention from telling my story?" "Am I playing games so I need help?" "Am I trying to prove my experiences were worse than anyone else's?" "Am I trying to fix the world so I don't have to change?" "Am I afraid of continuing my Life Journey?"

If you're not sure, but you think you could be stuck, listen to yourself. Stay aware of your words when you talk. Ask yourself the following questions:

Have I said this before?

Have I repeated these words so often that I don't have to pay attention to what I'm saying?

Do I wait for an opportunity to repeat these words?

Do I get a reaction from others that in some way "rewards" me and encourages me to repeat these words to other people?

Do people interrupt me and say "You already told me about this?"

If you answer "yes" to any one of these questions, you may want to ask yourself some specific questions about being stuck. Frequently the reason an individual continually repeats his anecdotal stories is he is trying desperately to get himself to listen. Everyone in his life has heard the experience but him. Often an individual cannot hear himself because he is too afraid of facing the real pain of the experience he is talking about. If the individual has not heard his own story he will be compelled to repeat it again and again both experientially and verbally.

It is a momentous moment in a person's life when he learns how to truly listen to himself. There are different approaches for listening to yourself. A very effective approach is to journal; to write down your thoughts and feelings about situations and watch for the patterns where you repeat yourself. Another approach is to quiet your mind and body and play the experience over and over on your mental screen until you allow the emotions to be quietly freed and dissipate. Still another approach is to tell a friend. A friend is someone who hears your song and sings it back to you when your voice falters. But, be respectful of your friends. Many people have literally worn out friends by telling them the same story over and over again. Brave friends may attempt to call your attention to the "pattern," but it's your personal responsibility to listen to yourself. Even if you have an incredibly good friend who can tell you when you are stuck, it's important not to abdicate your own responsibility for listening to your words and your experience.

Continually feeding your dragons negative emotions will also prevent you from being your Real Self, as will focusing your attention on solving other people's problems. Denial, blaming others for your problems, trying to control others, trying to get people to do things your way or to believe your beliefs, are all behaviors which prevent people from claiming their Real Selves.

One of the most insidious roadblocks to Real Self is often missed. This subtle yet powerful roadblock is called "wanting." Many find themselves trapped by their own "wanting." A woman wants a higher paying job. A man wants a promotion. A child wants a bike. An old person wants his youth. A young person wants to be an adult. A large woman wants to be petite. A petite woman wants to be tall. What is it that you want?

There is nothing wrong with wanting. The roadblock to Real Self occurs when "wanting" instead of authenticity becomes the focal point of the individual's attention. "Wanting" places the individual's focus in the future. You may even hear people say:

"When I get through with college, then I'll be happy."

"When I have a baby, then I'll be satisfied."

"When I find a man and get married, then I'll be complete."

"When I find the right boss who appreciates me, then I'll be content."

"When my children are grown, then I'll be pleased."

"When I get promoted, then I'll be able to take better care of myself."

Look at the basic sentence again and fill in the blanks for yourself.

When I _____ then I'll be _____.

This sentence tells volumes about an individual's roadblocks to being Real Self. The "When I" phrase tells us about the experience which is outside of the individual. This outside event must occur before the individual can "be". The sentence could actually read: When an event outside of myself occurs then I'll allow myself to "be" who I am. The problem is that there is always another event which must occur. Our "wanting" prevents us from focusing on being who we are in the moment.

For years I said, "When I finish this project then I'll be able to rest and take better care of myself." But after each project there was always another one. I never got to the rest of the sentence, "then I'll be." I was so involved in "wanting" events outside myself to be different that I put my "being," my life, on hold.

Reality is, no one ever gets totally what he wants. Not getting what we want doesn't injure or harm us. What does harm us is not being able to see "who we are" because we are so busy "wanting" things to be different than they are.

This doesn't mean we shouldn't work to make our lives and the world better. It does mean that wanting the world to be different and not "being" until that happens is a waste of a good life.

Over the years, I developed my own list of what prevents me from being authentic. I created this as a method of keeping truth with myself. I've also found there are specific situations which impel me to pretend not to be who I am. You may find it helpful to develop your own list of what prevents you from being authentic and the common situations in which it happens.

WHAT PREVENTS ME FROM BEING MY REAL SELF?

I prevent myself from being my Real Self when I do not accept myself for who I am.

I prevent myself from being my Real Self when I am not willing to accept others for who they are, when I want others to be different for my sake.

I prevent myself from being my Real Self when I am not truthful in my relationships.

I prevent myself from being my Real Self when I stop myself from living the moments of my life because I have unreal expectations or because I want the world to be different.

I prevent myself from being my Real Self when I do not take personal responsibility for determining my life.

I prevent myself from being my Real Self when I am not accountable for my own thoughts and actions.

I prevent myself from being my Real Self when I get so caught up in things that I forget who I am and become unable to find the natural joy in a sunset, a snow fall, petting a dog, in hugging a loved one, etc.

This is my list. What would you add or subtract? If you can determine what prevents you from being your Real Self, you will have discovered the next step on your journey.

You can also use the map in figure 1 to assist you in determining what prevents you from being your Real Self. To use this map as a metaphor, you will want to quiet your mind. Then, quiet your body and spend some time in your quiet place. When you are ready, leave your quiet place and begin the journey. Imagine, in your mind's eye, the clothes you will wear for the journey.

Imagine yourself walking around in the forest. Pay close attention to what you see. Is there light in the forest? What kind of trees do you see? What else do you notice? Imagine yourself walking toward one of your dragons. What does he or she look like? Will your dragon talk with you and explain his or her behavior?

After a period of time, leave the forest of daily life patterns and walk by the dragons who guard the road of awareness. As you stand on the path, you will see the Bridge of Choice. What is the bridge made of? How large is the bridge? Look across the bridge and you will see someone waiting on the other side. This person has been waiting for a very long time. This person is very wise. If you look closely you probably can make out a form.

Start to cross the bridge. As you cross the bridge, the person waiting on the other side will become more and more visible. This person represents your Wisdom. Approach this person. Ask this person what prevents you from being Real? Then be silent and wait for the answer. When the wise person has answered you, prepare to leave. Thank the person for talking with you. Tell the person you'd like to talk more in the future. Then, look at the feet of the wise person. There is a present there, waiting for you. It is a gift from your wise person. Open it. Look carefully at your gift. Contemplate the meaning of this gift.

When you are ready, return to your quiet spot and spend a few minutes unpacking everything you learned about yourself.

This internal exercise often has remarkable results. Every image, every feeling, every part of the internal experience is symbolic of the person's life. Sometimes, people find themselves in dark forests which are symbolic of an inner wish to shed more light on the daily life patterns. Sometimes, the dragons talk of how lonely and tired they feel as they try to offer continuous protection.

Some people say they must use this exercise several times before they can cross their bridge to their wise person. This is symbolic of the work the people must do before they are ready to listen. When people do talk with the wise person, they usually receive concise often delphic messages. One individual was told to make friends with her dragons. Another individual was told to pay more attention to her physical self. Still another was told to "let go." Each of these messages was very meaningful to the individual who received it.

The presents are wondrous clues to who you are and what prevents you from being your Real Self. The first present I ever received from my wise person was a jewelry box containing a diamond scepter and a ruby heart. The diamond is the symbol for value. The brilliant white color is symbolic of spirituality. The scepter is a symbol for power. Red symbolizes emotions and the heart is symbolic of bliss. When I put it all together it read: your personal power comes from your spirituality; value this and trust your heart to lead you to your bliss.

Others have told me about a range of presents. One person told me she received a mouse as a present. After much thought, she realized she was being mousey and diffident about her life. Her wise person was asking her to make choices. Another person disclosed he received a white flower which was his message to reveal the caring side of himself to his family. Whatever you receive as a gift, be sure to allow yourself the time to contemplate what this gift means to you.

Once you determine what is preventing you from being your Real Self, you will know your next step in the journey. Then, all you have to do is have the courage to take it. As the journey continues, you may lose your way. Don't worry. Whenever you don't know the next step, just quiet your mind and your body. Go to your quiet place and dress yourself for the journey. Then step into your forest of daily life patterns, talk with your dragons, cross the bridge of choice and visit your wise person. Do this until you determine your next step.

These types of exercises gently develop greater awareness. This type of awareness allows you to make better choices for your life. Making better choices in your life leads to greater self trust. Greater self trust generates the courage to be REAL.

And so, in these seven chapters I have offered you a map of the inner life journey. I can't guarantee its accuracy. The inner life journey has little to do with accuracy. But if you listen reverently, you'll be able to hear your own song and it will guide you.

RESOURCES

To obtain the instruments mentioned in this book, contact your local Carlson Learning Network Associate or Carlson Learning Company, Carlson Parkway, P.O. Box 59159, Minneapolis, Minnesota 55459-8247, (612) 449-2856

Other recommended materials from Carlson Learning Company:

The Mysteries of Motivation by Michael O'Connor and Sandra Merwin

The Values Conflict Action Planner by Michael O'Connor and Sandra Merwin

The Classical Styles Audio Album by Michael O'Connor and Sandra Merwin

FOR MORE INFORMATION ABOUT

- Sandra Merwin's lectures and workshops

- Quantity discounts for bulk purchases of this book

Contact:

TigerLily Press
4655 Baker Road
Minnetonka, MN. 55343